Families
and
Social
Intelligence

C. Margaret Hall

Llumina Press

Families and Social Intelligence *is a guide to discovering the power and complexity of families and social influences, as well as the impacts they have on our freedom and opportunities. This book is dedicated to readers who want to better themselves, their families, and the world we live in.*

Table of Contents

Why Families are Important

I. Families as Emotional Systems

M ost of us invest some of our strongest positive and negative feelings or emotions in our families. Consequently we often have clearly defined, compelling views about what our families should be like, or how our families and others' families need to be in order for us to do well in life. The sheer frequency and pervasiveness of these shared investments of personal feelings in our families means that we cannot easily avoid our families' emotional intensities, even though many families may appear to have both distant and close relationships.

Because of these basic family characteristics, it is useful to think of families as repositories of some of our most powerful feelings and deepest emotions. We essentially cannot easily resist getting emotionally involved in our closest personal relationships, in the behavior of members of the youngest generations of our families, or in applying our preferred family values to our own family situations. One result of this fact is that our daily lives may frequently evoke emotions that are at odds with each other, so that we feel constantly in turmoil or in conflict about our families, personal relationships, and seemingly unrelated matters. These internal conflicts are often the lived effects of marked gaps between our family ideals and our everyday realities, especially with respect to our families.

Families can usefully be thought of as emotional systems due to these dynamics of interdependence, and because each family creates its own boundaries between itself and other families, as well as between itself and communities. The different generations of families have the potential to form extended kin groups, which may or may not be actively connected to their related nuclear families. The variability in the relationships that families have between their nuclear families and their extended kin groups means that whole families may or may not be single groups of interacting family members. However, even when there are disconnections between nuclear families and their kin groups, the systemness of their emotional interdependence, as well as the personal bonds among family members in different generations of families, are ever ready to come into play, depending on circumstances. For example, the dynamic connections of family emotional systems may be activated temporarily by recounting some of the conditions or players in specific family histories.

Each family member is deeply embedded in the most frequently recurring patterns of interaction in that person's family or intimate group. Some of the patterns of emotional intensity, which characterize families, result from accumulations of exchanges among family members over long periods of time, often throughout the entire life-spans of individuals or several generations of family members. Thus we bond with our relatives more than with other individuals, largely because we interact with them through thick and thin, and throughout the longest continuing periods of time in our lifetimes.

The emotional systems of our families may be coherent, visible, and easy to identify as family relationships, or sufficiently fragmented so that they do not appear to be what most people think of as families. Although blood links are the shared basis of many family relationships, legal contractual bonds, or repetitions of interpersonal behavior through habit and custom, may create equally enduring family connections. Emotional relationships within our families are not held together by genetic or physiological similarities, but rather by repeated patterns of behavior in our everyday family exchanges.

Many of us strive to keep our families in some kind of balance, with the result that our comings and goings in relation to our families become more or less predictable. We habitually or deliberately develop routines, rituals, and clear expectations of ourselves and other family members, in order to provide sufficient stability and meaning in our everyday lives. However, even though we have to be protected and nurtured by our families at different stages of our lives, their routines and rituals may become so entrenched or so unique that they are experienced as being remote from our basic survival needs, or from our needs for family meanings.

Some of the conditions which determine qualities of relationships in family emotional systems include contrasts in families' closeness, tensions in interdependence, conflicts between families' shared needs and individuals' quests for autonomy, contrasts in kin connections among different generations, and ongoing assessments of what it means to be both free and responsible with respect to our families. Each of these major concerns is examined in this introductory chapter of *Families and Social Intelligence* in order to understand why families are so important to us, as well as to show how social intelligence can guide us to interact with our families more effectively and more meaningfully.

Family Closeness

In considering and dealing with the importance of families in our own lives, in societies, and throughout the world, we need to appreciate the necessity of achieving some kind of balance in our family emotional systems, in order that we should survive and do well. Social intelligence helps us to recognize critical differences between productive family closeness, for example, and the more destructive, suffocating family togetherness that may have harmed past family members, and could continue to damage present or future family members.

A frequently-given conventional answer to why our families are important to us is that they give us much desired and much needed support in our unfriendly, anonymous modern society. Although this view of families may be meaningful, the assumptions usually made about the benign nature of family closeness deny important negative characteristics of family togetherness, which need to be both understood and neutralized. For example, one of our most imperative existential individual and social needs is to be able to think clearly. Thus it behooves us to be aware that too much family togetherness can paralyze or impede our thought processes. When we become overly involved with our relatives' opinions, we tend to allow our relatives' dominance and guidance to take over, or even to obliterate our own initiatives. Furthermore, the conflict that frequently flows from our attempts to be our own selves in our families usually occurs when our families have high degrees of togetherness.

A sad consequence of the impairing influences of family togetherness is that when we lose our autonomy, due to the intensity of the emotional closeness of our relatives, we restrict our capacities to live fully. However, our families necessarily continue to be important to us because they enable us to carve out our own individualities, even though they at the same time challenge our very existence as individuals, due to the inhibiting and restrictive powers of their togetherness. Sometimes we try to adapt to our family togetherness influences by second guessing our own actions, particularly because we do not want to offend those who are near and dear, and we do not want to upset the emotional investments our relatives have made in their expectations for us. In doing this, we often choose to accommodate our families' demands because we find it difficult to cope with family scorn, and the threatened or actual withdrawal of comfortable family closeness and support.

Although family closeness is an ideal for many of us, it necessarily brings hazards that are difficult to both recognize and challenge. Social intelligence is a tool which combats the strong pressures to conform generated by our families because, in the long run, the loss of our selves and identities is too high a price to pay for indulging in the coziness of our families' togetherness. Life necessitates some fight for our survival and fulfillment, and when we cannot think clearly about which major interests we should express in order to thrive, we often do not lead the kinds of meaningful lives which we truly prefer.

Unfortunately our continuing needs for some degree of family closeness often result in our becoming entrapped in family relationships which are too tight for comfort, or too restrictive for independent action. In these circumstances, our social intelligence helps us to create and nurture more flexible family bonds, which allow us to come and go relatively freely in relation to our families' emotional systems. When we can both enjoy some family togetherness, and exercise autonomy, we find a new kind of family balance that allows all our family members to thrive.

Recognizing this social reality—that we should be challenged, but not overwhelmed, by our relatives' emotional investments in us—motivates us to start our journeys to build a healthier balance, or openness, in our families' closeness. When considering the needs of our young and elderly relatives, we see that encouraging and preserving the autonomy of our most dependent family members is just as essential—if not more so—as encouraging and preserving the autonomy of our most independent family members. Having the freedom necessary to live our lives fully is essential to building or maintaining strong families, as well as vital to securing a viable balance in our families' closeness.

Interdependence

Human beings are interdependent, or dependent on each other. This is shown most graphically by identifying different patterns of interaction in our families. Interdependence can also be thought of as a primary human condition, the core of society and social organization, and a fact of life that cannot be ignored. Interdependence is such a strong influence in our lives, that denying the depth of our basic needs for others imperils our existence.

Families and Social Intelligence

Families are important because we meet several of our vital survival needs—such as protection, nourishment, and procreation—through their interdependent strategies. However, sometimes we are negative about these particular functions of families, because we confuse the value our cultures place on family togetherness with the life-protecting tasks of family divisions of labor. This confusion stops us from seeing those patterns of family interdependence that are essential for our survival. When family closeness is confused with the more basic family interdependence, we may mistakenly believe that we can conduct our lives more effectively by separating from our families, or even by living in isolation from them.

Interdependence permeates all exchanges within our families, including our connections to our kin groups. In considering the importance of families in their own right, we need to acknowledge the moving force of interdependence in nuclear family interactions, as well as in transactions between nuclear and extended kin members. The overall organizing principle of interdependence affects both small group family structures, such as nuclear families of parents and children, and larger groups of extended family kin from both paternal and maternal lines of descent. This principle of interdependence determines, at least to some extent, the quality of the past and ongoing connections between nuclear families and their extended kin.

Understanding the importance of families, from the point of view of social intelligence, assumes some working knowledge of the primacy of interdependence in family emotional systems. Social intelligence shows that individuals are strongly influenced by the emotional quality of the interdependence in their families, and that family relationships often tend to be relatively closed rather than open. Some of the most influential contrasts in open and closed family relationships are described in the following section of this chapter of *Families and Social Intelligence*. Later in *Families and Social Intelligence*, increasing social intelligence is presented as one of the most effective ways to deal with problematic closed family relationships. For example, readers learn how to cope with issues of overly close interdependence in their families, and how to open up some of the most difficult-to-deal-with patterns of overly close interdependence in their own families.

One way in which we become more aware of the importance and influence of interdependence in our families is through experiencing the loss of a relative. When a loved one dies, for example, this loss often causes an upheaval in a family's already established interdependent relationships. Because some family members are necessarily more significant than others within particular family emotional systems, family members who are in the most critical positions in family exchanges—or who are the most active players in patterns of family interdependence—create the deepest losses in their families when they die.

Our family interdependence is also acted out in all our families' divisions of labor, and social intelligence increases our awareness of the wide range of possible family divisions of labor. Social intelligence helps us to see that traditional customs, entrenched social habits, and widely held cultural assumptions about divisions of labor do not necessarily define optimal ways to express our interdependence in our families, especially given the fact that we have many alternative choices about how to divide our family chores, and how to express our interdependence.

Divisions of labor assume some degree of teamwork among family members in order to achieve specific tasks. For example, interdependence in families is often thought of as emerging from family members' responsibilities to meet their ongoing survival and maintenance needs. Although family interdependence is not synonymous with family divisions of labor, feasible divisions of labor necessarily express patterns of interdependence.

Other patterns of family interdependence include family conflicts, inequalities among family members, power struggles in relationships, and reactivity between functioning and dysfunctioning family members. In some respects any patterns in family exchanges express interdependence among family members, so the question of how to use social intelligence to maintain balanced and healthy interdependence in families is significant.

Open and Closed Families

Open and closed relationship systems in families have different consequences for their family members. Open family relationships foster functional behavior among their family members, whereas closed family relationships increase different kinds of dysfunctional behavior among family members. Although most families fall somewhere between this range of open or closed family relationships, being able to assess contrasts between open and closed family systems helps us to increase our social intelligence, and to deal more effectively with our own and others' families.

Open families have more flexible relationships, which allow their family members considerable freedom to be themselves, and to do what they want to do. Thus members of open families come and go in relation to their families much more easily than members of closed families. Also, the openness of these families extends most importantly to members of their kin groups, with the result that members of the nuclear and extended families in the same family emotional system more easily maintain meaningful contacts with each other in their open families.

By contrast, closed families have more rigid, brittle relationship bonds that are easier to splinter, which restrict their family members' autonomy by their tightness. Members of closed families cannot come and go in relation to their families without causing considerable upset to their families' regimented ways of doing things. Closed families also often have a great deal of emotional distance between members of their nuclear and extended kin groups, so that family members in these relationship systems tend to dysfunction.

Social intelligence serves as a reliable guide for individuals who want to open up their family networks, so that their families can neutralize their relatively closed ways of doing things. When this happens, the formerly closed family relationships are brought into a new kind of balance, which is more realistic and more satisfying. Relatives who were previously trapped in patterns of relatively dysfunctional behavior can now achieve and maintain autonomy as a high priority in their day-to-day behavior.

In addition, open families are usually more connected to community groups and other social arenas in the wider society than closed families. Members of open families tend to be more responsible citizens, or more enlightened professionals and workers, for example. By contrast, because so much of members' emotional energy in closed families is taken up with maintaining the rigid structures of their families, members of closed families usually perform less well in societies.

Openness in families is an important ideal to strive for, because open exchanges produce an emotional climate that supports the creativity and continued well-being of all family members. Although open families are frequently more a dream than a reality, this is a meaningful and effective direction to take when we deliberately apply our social intelligence to our families. Individual contributions toward opening up family relationship systems benefit all family members, especially in the long run. Furthermore, individual family members' contributions to society, which are launched from foundations of open family relationships, benefit more members of society than is possible from bases of closed family relationships.

Social intelligence shows us that there are particular occasions when we can more easily intervene, and begin working toward opening up family relationships. These opportunities frequently occur during or after family crises, and at other critical turning points in our families' histories. Family crises have the emotional power to dislodge closed relationship systems, for example, and possibilities for changing closed family systems increase when there is some degree of disruption in families' usual routines. Shifts in family relationships necessarily take place after deaths, during or after geographical moves, and when additional family members are absorbed into families—a newborn child, an adopted child, a returning long-lost relative, or a dysfunctional family member who is well again. This loosening of rigidity in closed families makes family members more aware of a wider range of possible behavior choices.

The issue of open and closed families illustrates how families are important in different ways. If closed family relationship systems persist, without being modified, the tendencies of their family members to dysfunction increase. Because these conditions are difficult for closed family members to control or change, their life chances are diminished. Furthermore, chronically closed families cannot benefit from the support and stability which more connections to their kin groups could bring. Rather, closed families that do not change inevitably increase their estrangement from their kin groups, which ultimately impinges on the development of members of both current and future generations. In addition, the frequently found intense estrangement between nuclear families and their kin groups in closed families makes their nuclear families more easily overloaded with emotions, which may lead to their breakdown.

Needs and Autonomy

So what is it that pulls us and our families into patterns of closeness, interdependence, openness, or closedness? How are the importance of families and family emotional systems connected to our family dynamics and broad social influences? What makes social intelligence such a vital catalyst in controlling some of the unwelcome encroachments that most families make on our individualities? Are families the only social groups that can deal effectively with our shared human needs, or are there alternative viable ways in which society can meet our needs and desires for autonomy?

One answer to these questions is that families are enduring groups that meet individual and social needs to survive and prosper. Aspects of such deep-seated needs are people's desires for protection from the vicissitudes of the world; necessities

I. Families as Emotional Systems

such as dealing with hunger and sexuality; and requirements for the adequate care of young, old, sick, weak, or vulnerable family members. These desired ends or goals become shared responsibilities, and families continue to be the only arena where many responsibilities for others are both assumed and met. These real, deep-seated needs generate both togetherness among family members, and contrasting diffusive, fragmenting patterns of behavior. Furthermore, the extent to which we are needed to meet our own and relatives' needs strongly influences the many ways in which we may become trapped in our families' dependence for decades or more.

Social intelligence shows us that we survive the struggle for life by becoming our own selves, by maturing, by assuming family responsibilities, and by making constructive contributions to our own families and to society. Our urges to stay alive and to live fully motivate us to transcend some of our dependencies, so that we can become relatively independent amidst the ever present interdependence of our family emotional systems.

Ideally these tensions between family togetherness, and our individual strivings for accomplishment, are balanced by constructive family interactions throughout all the generations of our families. Open families accomplish this by maintaining meaningful contacts throughout their family emotional systems. Consequently, standing squarely on the strong emotional foundations of open families, allows us to be more autonomous and more creative in our exchanges with relatives and members of societies.

When considering divisions of labor in families, as means to meet basic responsibilities for daily sustenance, it is easy to conclude that it is the particular roles we play that meet dependency needs. However, the tasks that family members perform, such as parenting, are necessarily superficial means to understand the depth of our most intimate personal needs, as well as our real strivings for autonomy. It is more practical to approach and assess family members' actions from the point of view of their shared needs to balance family responsibilities.

Furthermore, once we meet our own and our relatives' needs throughout our families, we can address broader social needs and social justice more adequately.

Our ongoing challenges to meet our family responsibilities —even when our relatives' needs appear to be impossibly bottomless or never-ending—also require that we balance our tendencies to be either over-responsible or irresponsible. Responsible action is achieved when we balance our needs and our autonomy in relation to others' needs and autonomy.

As we strive to balance our needs and autonomy, we have to avoid becoming martyrs, who make themselves ever available for significant others in their families, or for people in other social settings. It is more responsible to muster the courage necessary to move into unknown, even treacherous social territories, so that we can make more constructive, creative contributions to others. Social intelligence suggests that we should try to respond to others' real needs, but at the same time make sure that we act as equal team players in meeting routine tasks in our families, and in participating in major family events. Consequently, when we make a high priority of continuing to balance our needs and autonomy successfully, we are less likely to get trapped in others' definitions of roles that they insist we should play.

Achieving a satisfactory balance between our needs and our autonomy enables us to have more objectivity about our lives. This is essential for continuing to build our social intelligence, which also helps us to maintain realistic perspectives on what is truly significant in our families and in the rest of our lives.

Kin Connections

The power and importance of families are more fully realized when we make connections between our inner circle family members and members of our extended families. When we think only of the conventional nuclear constellations of parents and children as our families, we see and experience a truncated view of our families' real power and importance.

I. Families as Emotional Systems

In modern industrialized societies—particularly in Western cultures—extended family kin usually have reduced capacities to realize both their family power and their emotional importance. However, social facts suggest that these abilities are dormant, and that critical bonds between nuclear families and their kin groups can be reactivated or activated at any time. Moreover, it is only those families which manage to stay or get connected to their kin groups that are truly emotionally strong and powerful within themselves and in societies.

Bonding with extended family kin is perhaps most obviously beneficial for increasing the economic strength of families, which is usually measured by the amount of shared resources gained. Less obvious, but often more important, is that bonding with extended family kin is a reliable source of increased emotional strength. First, family emotional systems stay open or become open when they include meaningful relationships with a sufficient number of extended family kin. Second, the expanded range of relationships experienced through members of kin groups increases the restricted quantity and quality of diversity in nuclear families. A fuller embrace of kin diversity is achieved through deliberately making increased contacts with relatives of different ages, different religions, different races and ethnicities, different social classes, different occupations, and varied personal styles.

By contrast, relationships in nuclear families easily become overloaded and strained by meeting only their own basic needs, and by maintaining only their own intense emotional relationships in their relatively closed emotional networks. A predictably beneficial strategy, which reduces nuclear family tensions in closed families, is to open up the nuclear groups through contacting a wide range of members of their extended kin groups. The more kin members are included in the nuclear family emotional systems, the more the nuclear families open up, and the more meaningful relationships are among both nuclear family members and kin members. This opening up of nuclear family emotional systems stabilizes and strengthens the whole family, and family members predictably function better than before throughout their broadened emotional relationship systems.

Family dynamics suggest that the more comprehensive the networks of nuclear and extended families are, the more the nuclear-kin connections enable family members to thrive. For example, a broad-based family emotional system allows young children to mature in more holistic ways, while elders benefit from gaining access to more support when needed. Kin connections broaden the emotional bases of nuclear families, and at the same time increase possibilities for the autonomy of all family members. By contrast, where there are many estrangements, or poor communications, between nuclear and extended family members, problematic patterns of behavior develop and persist.

Sometimes the most practical way to open up closed nuclear families is to bridge specific historical emotional cut-offs in the relationships between members of nuclear families and their kin group members. For example, people make greater progress in opening up their nuclear families when they focus on building meaningful relationships with those kin group members who have been the most estranged, rather than on establishing random kin connections. Seeking out the most emotionally distant member of a family's kin group, and trying to build a meaningful relationship with this person, brings considerable emotional rewards to the whole family, such as increasing the emotional stability of the family system, and increasing the flexibility of family relationships.

Kin groups offer nuclear families increased cultural diversity, increased opportunities to understand a wide range of people, and increased resources. In Eastern cultures, where extended family kin relations are, and have been, the norm or standard for most families, there may be more problems around the control of economic resources and power. These conflicts of interest may not be as apparent in Western cultures, where the social, economic, and power dimensions of kin groups have declined rapidly, or been denied, during the last few centuries. However, in both West and East, when nuclear and kin relations are on a relatively equal footing—with a more or less balanced give-and-take among the different age groups in the nuclear and extended family systems—the emotional anchor of kin groups enhances possibilities and opportunities for all family members.

This process of being connected, or getting connected, with kin members is often difficult to initiate or establish. Connecting and maintaining kin relationships may take enormous amounts of time, energy, and resources, for example. Furthermore, newly forged connections with kin members easily disappear if they are not maintained regularly. However, a reassuring note is that links with kin relatives remain at least dormant or latent, and they can be relatively easily activated by intentional actions at any time, especially when there is a family celebration—such as a wedding or a birth—or a family loss—such as a death.

Toward Freedom
It is especially through our families that we attain important freedom. Even though our families represent, for many of us, a mass of ever-changing responsibilities, or close relationships which are frequently difficult to deal with, families are at the same time our toughest and our truest testing grounds for defining who we are. It is through the complex and powerful emotional systems of our family relationships that we experience our strongest challenges to our daily decisions about self and others.

Our family emotional systems help us to experience and understand the most overwhelming obstacles we face in trying to actualize what it is that we really want to achieve. We easily become over-responsible, for example, when we assume too many leadership roles in our families, or when we try to control our most intimate others. Also, if we become ensnared by family dependency issues, or by family control dynamics, we can spend decades repeating unproductive behavior patterns. It is particularly our emotional dependencies that cloud our visions of how we can give back most effectively to our families and societies, or of what our families and societies could be like.

Gaining freedom—or even gaining the slightest incremental increase in our freedom—is an important goal for all of us, whether we recognize this or not. Finding self, through our complex family connections, enables us to connect with others by making commitments to broader social causes, thereby contributing to societies and the global community. Some of the preliminary steps needed before this can happen include seeing the vital, necessary parts families and freedom play in achieving individual fulfillment and a more inclusive common good.

Freedom can be assessed by examining how we think, how we respond to our feelings, how willing we are to assume responsibilities, and how committed we are to making the world a better place. Living in purely individualistic ways, and considering only self-centered goals, cannot increase our freedom and creativity in the long run. Only when we understand why families are important to us all, can we use social intelligence to guide us effectively in more expansive directions.

Acquiring a research orientation to our families facilitates our individual journeys toward freedom. We need to take careful note of how our family members interact with us, for example, and of how we react to our most significant others. Assessing whether our families are emotionally close or distant, gives us a more realistic context or baseline for making changes in ourselves and in our families. Furthermore, we need to continuously monitor the degrees and kinds of interdependence expressed in our families, in order to come to terms with our own behavior, as well as with possibilities for changes in our families. We must be able to see how our own open or closed families affect our basic needs and abilities to be autonomous, as well as the quality of our relationships with our kin groups.

These particular family patterns are not easily discerned, especially because our observations should be sustained for long periods of time, in order to be sure that we recognize and appreciate the importance of our families' influences on our behavior. The ways in which we think, respond to our feelings, assume responsibilities, and make commitments all result from how we interact with the complex networks of our family emotional systems.

The structures and patterns of behavior that we consider as unique in our own families are important influences on how we define our beliefs and our life chances. However, our beliefs, decisions, and actions are also related to broad social influences such as religions, social classes, cultures, politics, and history. Because our families necessarily filter or distort these broad social influences, their impacts on us are variable.

Whatever the effects of religions, social classes, cultures, politics, and history are, we need to be able to stand up for ourselves in our own families—and in our societies—whenever necessary, especially if we see things differently from our relatives and other people. Ideally, the emotional tensions and emotional conditioning of our families prepare us to deal more effectively with differences of opinions and beliefs in the wider society. This means that one of the most essential legacies we can give—to future generations of our relatives and to societies—is to heighten youngsters' awareness of who they are, of what they can expect from their families and societies, and of how they can make their most effective contributions to the common good.

II. Families and Beliefs

O ur beliefs influence our families a great deal, because our strongest commitments motivate us to establish our goals and priorities, and to act upon them. However, our beliefs also interact with our perceptions, which may be at odds with reality. This means that we must do whatever we can to check the reliability of our beliefs, with facts and our own experiences. Unfortunately, there are often sizable gaps between what we believe, and the realities we face and deal with on a daily basis.

Although some alignments may be made between our personal beliefs and our religions or faiths, social intelligence shows us that wide ranges of both sacred and secular beliefs influence who we are, who we want to be, and what we do. These sacred and secular beliefs or world views, which may be political or cultural, derive from social sources. However, before looking more closely at the varieties of possible beliefs that influence what we do, we need to acknowledge and take into account the power and force that religious beliefs may have.

When values within a particular religious faith are treated as sacred—such as codes of conduct, or traditions around sexuality and marriage—we frequently succumb to that religion's powerful prohibitions or sanctions, especially when we align our deepest personal beliefs with these same religious values. When our beliefs in the power of a supernatural being overwhelm us, we necessarily believe that we are—by contrast—relatively powerless, especially when we act in accordance with sacred tenets based on the ultimate power of this supernatural being. Thus religious beliefs may play very significant parts in the repertoires of our beliefs, especially in our beliefs about our selves and our families.

Our family relationships and family dynamics usually dictate which religions we are socialized into, and who leads and directs our religious upbringing. Furthermore, those parents or relatives who make decisions about families' religious observances—particularly when there are young children in these families—are frequently dominant in many patterns of family behavior. Therefore, when we become adults, we benefit from understanding how we absorbed our religious beliefs, how our family dynamics influenced our religious upbringing, and why we continue to emphasize those particular religious beliefs which we cherish the most.

In some important respects, our non-religious or secular beliefs may not be any weaker than our religious beliefs, and being socially intelligent requires that we unravel the many ways in which secular beliefs also affect our families and our lives. We become stronger to the extent that we can identify the social sources of as many of our beliefs as possible, so that we understand more fully how they influence our decisions and behavior.

As well as being influenced by social beliefs about social classes, cultures, and societies or political systems, we are indelibly—although sometimes imperceptibly—influenced by our families' unique belief systems. For example, what we think of as "natural" or "common sense" essentially results from the deep influences that our own families' values and beliefs have on our thinking and doing. What we take for granted in defining our life chances is largely whatever it is that we learned first from our families.

From the point of view of social intelligence, we can say that our families have specific belief systems that are held in place by patterns of family dependence, as well as by our families' emotional systems. These beliefs influence us at very deep levels, because they were integral parts of our religious and secular socialization as children. Family beliefs also influence the ways in which we eventually choose or reject our religious and secular beliefs as adults.

One of the harmful consequences of the beliefs we encounter and make our own is that they tend to crystallize over time, with the result that our everyday beliefs and behavior may become overly rigid and dogmatic. The intensity of our most clear-cut beliefs frequently makes us act in accordance with preconceived expectations. These essentially out-of-date beliefs also prevent us from cultivating the degree of flexibility needed in our beliefs, in order to make effective adaptations to our changing circumstances and opportunities. Rigid beliefs foster prejudice, discrimination, and bigotry in our interpersonal relations, both within our families and in societies. Thus we need to be aware that in their most extreme forms, our beliefs have the potential to either inspire us to make superhuman efforts to achieve heroic goals, or to compel us to commit despicable atrocities against humankind.

We shall look more closely at some of the varied social sources of our beliefs later in this chapter of *Families and Social Intelligence*. The principal advantage, of understanding more clearly what the social sources of our beliefs are, is that we can then move in directions that enable us to change our beliefs, especially beliefs which could be destructive to ourselves and others. In these respects, social intelligence guides us to make new kinds of decisions based on our own more deliberately chosen beliefs, ideals, and priorities.

Sources of Beliefs

Our families are important because they are the sources of many of our beliefs, including our beliefs about families. However, our beliefs about families are influenced not only by beliefs that we absorb from our families, but also by beliefs about families that we receive from other complex social sources, such as religions, social classes, cultures, and societies. These combined sources of our beliefs about families affect our priorities, our decisions, and our behavior because they underlie our understanding of ourselves and the world.

Families and Social Intelligence

Family and social sources of our beliefs about families do not usually transcend our past and present lived experiences. The origins of whatever we believe are embodied by people we have known the best throughout long periods of time, as well as by the most meaningful groups to which we have belonged. Furthermore, however religious or spiritual our beliefs may seem, they were not usually produced by divine interventions, but rather result from varied family and social interactions.

Those people who have been the most emotionally significant to us, and the groups with which we have interacted the most, have profound impacts on what we believe, who we believe we are, and what we decide to do with our lives, whether or not we accept or like this fact. In addition, our views about our families are influenced by many contemporary and past social groups beyond our families.

The social sources of our beliefs about our families reflect social structures, especially because we generally have statuses within particular groups, organizations, and institutions. We see the world, ourselves, and our families depending in part on our statuses in broad ranges of families, religions, social classes, cultures, and societies or political systems. In addition, values and views of families are found everywhere in our societies because they are crucial to the survival of all societies. Social intelligence helps us to recognize that we need to create stable and continuing families successfully, if we are to survive as individuals, families, and societies.

Our beliefs about families are at the core of our families, communities, and societies. These beliefs tie us—through our commitments—into reinforcing the importance of our families through our personal bonds, values, and behavior. Our interdependence and reciprocity make it difficult for us to change our deepest beliefs about our families, even though our beliefs about families may not be in our own or others' best interests.

Coming to terms with the intensity of our beliefs about families, and the impacts these beliefs have in meeting the ongoing day-to-day needs of our families, may challenge us for a lifetime. It is vital, for example, that we do not sacrifice our independence to relatives' pressures to conform to their family beliefs. However, only when we know what our own beliefs about families are, can we control the impact of some of the tensions and stresses of dealing with others' family beliefs. We need to know how to withstand social pressures to conform to particular models of families suggested by cultural norms and standards, how to resist ways of thinking that derive directly from religious or secular rationales about families, and how to control our own emotional reactivity to specific family beliefs and values.

Social intelligence enables us to see that many different aspects of society influence the development and well-being of our families. Even though families have their own unique belief systems, they are not exclusively formed by their own belief systems, or by beliefs that are held by most of their relatives. For example, current gender roles vary widely within society at large, and these patterns of gender behavior and gender interaction may have strong impacts on individual families. Similarly, national and international trends in demographic influences, such as birth rates, have differential impacts on our families.

Understanding more about the complexities of these broad patterns in widespread, contrasting family circumstances enables us to exercise more real choices about our own families, and makes it more possible to resist the influences of strong social expectations to conform to particular family patterns. Both acknowledging and accepting the social origins of our beliefs about families brings individual freedoms, as well as different kinds of responsibilities for our own families, and for other people's families.

Family Beliefs

Because families serve vital functions that are directly related to their own daily existence and survival, some widely held family beliefs develop and persist because of their abilities to meet members' individual and group needs. For example, an important family belief is that it is largely collective actions within families that protect all family members, and perpetuate their best chances to endure, especially in hazardous conditions. This belief, that families protect their members, is frequently evoked and expressed in times of family crises like childbirth or death, or to increase the material gain and success of their members, whether or not families have to deal with harsh economic realities.

Families are distinct small groups, which form their own social hierarchies. Furthermore, the power of individual family members may be more directly related to their emotional standing within a particular family, than to their financial resources, although sometimes these two characteristics coincide or overlap. Beliefs about individuals' and families' statuses evolve from family and societal hierarchies. For example, beliefs about sex and age in society—basic social hierarchies—may reinforce or challenge particular family expectations and responsibilities related to sex and age. The fact that women and men have culturally distinct gender roles in most societies, leads to certain gender-specific actions and attitudinal styles being supported and reinforced by individual families' beliefs. Similar patterns, related to age in society, influence family members' understanding of different ages, with added variations for women and men. Thus the pervasiveness and power of these family beliefs help to maintain sex and age role differences within families and in societies.

Families also develop their own cultures, which are influenced by religions, social classes, societal cultures, and political histories. For example, upwardly mobile families have different family beliefs from static or downwardly mobile families. Because the everyday beliefs of all families are emotionally significant influences on their family members' behaviors, these beliefs usually establish particular work habits and work ideals for a lifetime and for generations.

Leadership and dominance within families are inevitably reflected in their families' belief systems. Because it is not ideal

II. Families and Beliefs

for a family to have a few dominant members, the less dominant family members may try to dislodge established family beliefs, in order to create more inclusive distributions of power and rewards. When this is successful, and power and rewards are redistributed, more family members share these privileges. Consequently, new kinds of family beliefs become more explicit in these families' cultures, so that their hard-won family reorganization can be preserved.

The most significant family beliefs—those which have the most powerful and most durable effects on their family members—are those which incorporate views of human nature and the world. Family narratives about everyday behavior reflect the extent to which family members believe in the power of individual actions, for example, or the effectiveness of collective deliberations. Families who do not believe in the importance of creating and maintaining the autonomy of their members are less free than families who place high priorities on each family member being autonomous. These significant differences in the qualities of family beliefs either limit or increase the effectiveness of family members' actions in the world.

Other important characteristics of family beliefs are that they tend to be deep-seated and emotionally intense, frequently being supported by strong consensuses of family togetherness. When families are dominated by a few family members, their family beliefs are usually more rigid and more bigoted—and thus less beneficial—than the flexible beliefs of families which have more egalitarian relationships. Families that temper or moderate their shared beliefs, enhance life chances for their members more effectively, than families that are supported by less inclusive belief systems.

Whatever the specific beliefs families hold, ways to adapt and modify family beliefs are needed, because this kind of opening up of beliefs is synonymous with life itself. For example, maintaining family traditions through rigid family beliefs, may gradually lead to the extinction of some families in the long run, because the capacities of these families to make necessary adaptations to changes are reduced. By contrast, habitual intergenerational exchanges, which promote flexible family beliefs and flexible family bonds, strengthen families' capacities to survive, because these are successful family adaptations to broad societal changes.

Religious Beliefs

Many family beliefs are welded together and upheld through families' religious beliefs and practices. In this way the religious leaders of families can, it seems very legitimately, make selective uses of divine sanctions to uphold their own family beliefs. Although most people acknowledge the power and influence that religious beliefs may have on individual lives, or on the course of collective actions within a given society, unless sufficient social intelligence is exercised—individual or shared—there may be relatively little recognition of the fact that there are frequent connections between family beliefs and religious beliefs in many families and societies.

Religions have power and influence in their own right, regardless of the distortions of religious beliefs that may result from merging family beliefs with religious beliefs. Furthermore, when we examine religious beliefs in their broadest applications, we see that the major world religions and their sects may say and practice much that is more directly related to family interaction than to a sacred being, or to how a supernatural reality should be acknowledged in daily practices. Because of these interconnections we see that religions need families to recruit new members to their communities, especially children. Furthermore, religions maintain their links with families by prescribing sacrosanct norms for family behavior, and by proscribing family patterns which do not conform to their religious values.

In practical terms, religious beliefs relate directly to our most basic human life cycle needs: love, responsibilities, sexual relations, marriage, conception, pregnancy, births, child care, illness, elder care, and death. As well as outlining particular practices and rules to meet these basic individual and social needs of human beings, religions add sanctions of divine approval or disapproval to particular aspects of family or intimate behavior. Because moral values permeate the substance of religions' normative prescriptions, religious beliefs and teachings also strongly influence secular beliefs about good and evil in families, as well as in the world.

It is through the chosen religious practices of family leaders that children usually have their first encounters with religious values. Because religious beliefs encompass both family beliefs and societal beliefs, children in religious families may be held to standards and sanctions that make little sense to them. One of the most critical aspects of being raised in religious families, is that even though appeals to religious authority outside families may appear to strengthen the disciplinary impact of parents on their children, this does not necessarily bring cooperation from children in the long run. Children frequently rebel against what they experienced as coercions of religious sanctions, especially when they become adolescents or adults.

Religions are particularly concerned and involved with the early religious training of children, because they need to replace members of their congregations from generation to generation. Religions also have strong influences on our definitions of human potential, success in life, and world views. These areas are critical to human happiness, which means that religious beliefs—when accepted unquestioningly—can dictate much of what we think and do for ourselves and others in our everyday behavior.

Some of the qualities of character, that religious beliefs and religious teachings instill, include a respect for traditions of the past, and a reverence for divine inspiration in daily life. Children are led to believe that their elders know best, and that past ways of doing things should be revered rather than changed. For example, children in religious families are often praised for being quiet, orderly, and obedient. Religious training rarely encourages individual thinking and independent critiques of the status quo, as this kind of participation in religious and social communities challenges the ways things are done in congregations and at home, as well as established power hierarchies.

Social intelligence gives us more objective views of what is really going on between our families and our religions. Consequently, we have to ask ourselves moral and ethical questions about the extent to which both our families' beliefs and religious beliefs should be challenged. For example, is it not important for us to critically assess the status quo, so that we can create a more just world, rather than perpetuate conditions which may not work well for large numbers of people?

Unless these kinds of questions are raised about our families and our religious beliefs, human frailties may encourage meaningless transmissions of religious beliefs, which may actually harm the autonomy and confidence of members of the youngest generations in our families. Rather, we need to create breathing spaces in our family beliefs, as well as some emotional distance from our religious beliefs, so that we can develop sufficiently broad world views to ward off bigotry, prejudice, and discrimination. We want to pass on those religious values of the past that will predictably help to strengthen and renew our communities, increase social justice, and strengthen our motivations to achieve whatever is good or needed in our societies. Before we can accomplish these goals, however, we have to be truly educated about the social realities we share, and the ways in which we can realistically make the world a better place. We cannot exercise true moral choices and ethical responsibilities if we continue to accept those family beliefs and religious beliefs that family elders selectively endorsed for their own purposes.

Social Class Beliefs

For the purposes of considering why families are important to us, and how our families relate to social intelligence, it is useful to consider social classes as categories in which people are thought about collectively. Our ideas about social classes are influential, because how we categorize ourselves and others

II. Families and Beliefs

is directly connected to the ways in which we understand human nature and the world around us, and orients much of our decision-making and day-to-day behavior.

Today's social classes, or ways in which people are thought about collectively, include categories of stratification based on differences in economic means, educational achievement, gender, sexual orientation, race, ethnicity, and able-bodiedness. However, the most usual historical, traditional ways of thinking about social classes are based on assessments of individuals' and families' economic means and educational achievement.

Although we have choices about how salient this wide range of social class differences is in our own daily lives, we must first become aware of how others label us as belonging to particular social classes, as well as how we see ourselves. Life is a process of highly complex patterns of social interactions, and we must be prepared for others' responses to us if we are to live fully, as well as improve the social well-being of our families and others' families.

Our families are significantly defined by our social class affiliations. We know, for example, that living with physically handicapped family members affects patterns of family interaction very deeply, as well as ways in which societies respond to us as families. In this situation, and in other circumstances where we are labeled in particular ways by our communities, we need to be constantly aware of the choices we make in defining our perceptions, beliefs, and goals.

The historical, traditional social class bases of economic means and educational achievement are interrelated. In societies where inherited wealth is not widely available, most economic means are acquired thorough earning incomes, which are sometimes supplemented by financial investments from economic surpluses after basic family needs are met. Families' abilities, opportunities, and privileges, with regard to accumulating economic means, are also inevitably influenced by family members' education and acquired professional skills. Thus, we do well financially, and benefit from society's divisions of labor, when we achieve high levels of education in our modern, credential society.

The relentless predictability of our social classes sustains our social hierarchies, frequently in spite of our individual or collective aspirations to create societies with more egalitarian ideals and relationships. Very often our families are ranked in hierarchies as groups, without much attention to individual differences within families. However, in reality, the status or social mobility of a particular family may depend largely on the performance or dysfunction of one or two family members.

Similar ranking systems are well-established for social classes based on gender, sexual orientation, race, ethnicity, and able-bodiedness. When these class bases have clear visual indicators—such as gender, race, and physical disability—individuals find themselves not only being put into specific social classes by others, but at the same time being stereotyped. When visible characteristics are stereotyped negatively, individuals and their families are stigmatized, and may eventually suffer from life-changing consequences of prejudice and discrimination.

Even when social class characteristics are less visible to others—as in sexual orientation, ethnicity, and able-bodiedness—similar kinds of social hierarchies, prejudice, and discrimination may be evoked at any time. Thus we are not only victims of external appearances, but also of the potential stigmas that may develop from being "outed" in random or unpredictable ways. Given these powerful social influences in societies, what are the choices that individuals and families can make? How can individuals be more responsible in their particular social class situations, so that they work toward social justice rather than perpetuate prejudice, discrimination, and inequalities?

An initial step toward neutralizing some of the pernicious consequences of social classes is to become more aware of the complexity of overlapping social classes in contemporary societies, as well as throughout history. We need to size up the situations we are in as objectively as possible, if we are to reduce the destructive consequences of how social classes define our individual, family, and social well-being. Helping family members to think clearly about social class influences makes significant progress possible, so that we gradually move toward increasing autonomy in our families, increasing freedom in societies, and increasing social justice. Social intelligence guides us in making these meaningful journeys, and in facing these daunting challenges.

Cultural Beliefs

Whatever social class we are in—by our own definitions or through others' assignments—we also have strong shared experiences of being immersed in the most distinctive cultures of our societies. Social intelligence helps us to see how social classes affect our access and commitment to mainstream cultures, and how social class beliefs are maintained by cultural inclusion or exclusion from the rewards of being accepted as players in the dominant cultures of society.

Culture has significant power dimensions, which suggest that in order to be free agents in societies we must nurture beliefs that accept possibilities for change and empowerment. Because some cultural beliefs do not empower specific individuals and groups—especially those in lower economic social classes, or in some racial or ethnic groups—all cultural beliefs need to be questioned and modified. Individuals' senses of agency increase when their cultural beliefs and values are assessed as objectively as possible, as well as when they use social intelligence to guide their goals and actions toward constructing more inclusive cultures.

Religions, social classes, and cultures are important social sources of beliefs which emphasize the past, present, future, or life after death. Beliefs about whether individuals and groups should assume responsibility for societies' past, present, or future orient actions toward change, or toward maintaining the status quo. These orienting beliefs and values are found in cultures, as well as in religions, or in the experiences of non-mainstream groups. The more general and more secular bases of shared cultural beliefs help us to assume responsibilities for our individual and collective destinies, so that we are not fatalistic about being victims of religious or social class influences.

The strength and power of cultural beliefs is shown through cultures' almost infinite bases of shared values—often including capitalistic market values—and their capacities to cross national boundaries in globalization. Today, cultural values and beliefs cannot be understood merely as important parts of a single society, but rather as international forces.

These pervasive, almost inescapable aspects of our cultural beliefs need to be pondered, when we assess the influences of cultural beliefs on our families. Furthermore, we find that the substance or content of many cultural beliefs is frequently focused on family concerns, family issues, and family expectations. The images, ideals, and prescriptions for love and family life that are found in our cultures—especially in mass media—are strong influences on our dreams and aspirations for our own and others' families. Social intelligence helps us to see the inevitable gaps between cultural myths about families and individual and social family realities, especially in relation to family responsibilities and personal relationships.

One particularly pernicious cultural belief, that has already had a devastating effect on the quality of our family relationships throughout modern societies, is the emphasis given to romantic love in the nuclear family. This unrealistic idealizing of what it takes to build lasting relationships and strong families, and to rear healthy children, makes it very difficult for most people to understand the demanding responsibilities that are necessary for maintaining families. When false myths about romance diminish the importance of cultivating stamina and good judgment, for example, our personal relationships easily become emotionally overburdened, with the predictable result that many families break down.

By contrast, we benefit from cultural beliefs that shift emphasis away from romantic love, so that we can be more realistic about our families and relationships, as well as appreciate the importance and significance of staying connected to our families and their extended kin groups. Social intelligence shows us that families that include their extended kin members have broader bases of meaningful bonds, which serve as stable, dependable, ongoing foundations for meeting varied family and social needs.

Another aspect of modern Western culture, which is being rapidly exported world-wide through the global revolution in technology and information, is the magnification of cultural beliefs and stereotypes about families in the media. Whereas in the past public opinion, especially in local communities, was an extremely powerful and difficult cultural force for families to contend with, the former power of local community beliefs has now been largely replaced by broad cultural influences such as popular television programs and advertising, which often promulgate false images and unrealistic expectations for families.

Media stereotypes of families, and their related presentations of white middle class beliefs and values about families to audiences made up of all social classes and varied racial or ethnic backgrounds, bring problematic individual and social consequences. Troubling contemporary trends, such as the widening gap between wealthy and poor families, are influenced by these kinds of media representations and dynamics, so that the numbers of alienated and disenchanted individuals or groups in contemporary societies have increased. Because family breakdowns do not occur randomly or by chance, social intelligence can strengthen our capacities to change the impacts of harmful cultural influences, as well as help us to create more constructive cultures for our families.

Political Beliefs

Social intelligence encourages examinations of the most significant effects and limitations of political beliefs, in order to determine how political beliefs in traditional and modern societies affect individuals, families, communities, and societies. Political beliefs necessarily reflect and represent many of societies' most powerful influences on families and individuals, and they should be critically assessed and deliberately chosen in the same ways as our religious beliefs.

Populations of modern societies are usually aware that they are nation states, and generally have administrative and legal systems which manage their power relations and meet their societies' basic needs. Even though levels of political awareness within specific societies vary a great deal, and political regimes differ dramatically, some important similarities among widely held political beliefs can be discerned and analyzed. This is useful because some of the shared dimensions of widely held political beliefs have tangible consequences for family and individual well-being, as well as for societies.

Before focusing on political beliefs and families within our wider consideration of why families are important, it is worthwhile to remember that in a contemporary, global society the broadest social influences that affect us often go beyond the boundaries of individual nation states. For example, we are members of religious groups, races, ethnic communities, gender classes, and the global community in ways that often require us to transcend the basic parameters and limits of nation states. Because we are all citizens of planet earth, some understanding of world history, and even of evolution, is necessary to grasp the significance of the distributions of power and power relations in particular societies.

The complexity of these influences shows us that our political beliefs usually emerge as products of the distributions of power and power relations both within a society and beyond that society. Forging links between the local histories of individual families, and national or international trends in world history, helps us to grasp the impact of these broad social influences on families and individuals.

Families are vulnerable to political regimes in many ways, and for many reasons. Families need some degree of physical protection by nation states, if only at the level of maintaining conditions of peace rather than war, and of prosperity rather than poverty. Although planned family policies may not offer adequate solutions for many family problems, there is much agreement that what goes on in societies has deep impacts on family well-being. Therefore it is in our own interests to understand which family needs and social issues have to be dealt with, if we are to survive and have favorable opportunities in the best of all practical worlds.

Unless political beliefs support democratic principles, families are at the mercy of totalitarian rule. We need to live in societies where political beliefs in democracy are upheld, in order to legitimize and enjoy family well-being throughout our broadest kin groups. Beliefs in democracy pave the way for establishing freedoms within families and among families, as well as in societies.

Democratic rule, at least as an ideal, is based on beliefs which lead to the implementation of policies to equalize opportunities—in practical and meaningful ways—among all social classes, thereby leveling economic contrasts among groups in given societies. This approach to political beliefs and family well-being can also be thought of as a holistic approach to solving major family problems, which may be essentially economic, educational, or occupational.

Although a comprehensive orientation to achieving an accessible public good for all is laudable, we know from experience that high levels of agreement about the goals of social policies to benefit families do not necessarily ensure their adequate or efficient implementation. Our political beliefs and policies need to be rooted in acceptable practices, as well as ideals, in order to meet our most pressing family needs.

Families raise important issues in political beliefs, because families are needed by both societies and political parties. However, families often do not have effective political representations, or access to political power at the highest levels of decision-making and implementations of policies. Furthermore, political beliefs are usually fickle or changeable, so that they quickly become inadequate supports for families. Although societies need political beliefs to uphold ideals which are in families' interests, these are a necessary but not a sufficient condition for protecting families and individuals on a continuing basis.

III. Families and Social Class

As already mentioned in the preceding chapter, "Families and Beliefs," social classes can be thought of as being based on several different but separate criteria, rather than solely on varying amounts of economic assets, as has been customary after the industrial revolution in many Western societies. For example, although modern societies continue to organize significant social class distinctions on economic bases, widely accepted alternative ways of dividing social classes include variations in educational achievement, gender, sexual orientation, race, ethnicity, or able-bodiedness.

Before looking more closely at social classes based on economic resources and their relationships to educational achievement, gender and sexual orientation, and race and ethnicity, some attention should be paid to broad social influences which affect families and social classes. For example, family well-being is inextricably tied to the overall opportunity structures within social stratification systems, as well as to the social class origins of particular families. This means that we have to recognize and scrutinize contrasts in social castes, social mobility, divisions of labor, and power. These social conditions strongly influence the ways in which social classes affect families.

Social intelligence suggests that opportunity structures must be accessible and widespread in societies, if community, rather than alienation, characterizes social class relations. This means that unless families and family members can find ways to better themselves, or to have relatively equal access to societies' rewards, the predictable widespread discontent that follows ultimately results in alienation, crime, or violence.

Therefore, when we consider the impact that social classes have on families, we need to understand what the social consequences are of particular kinds of social class arrangements for the whole society, as well as for individual families. In so doing we must ask whether the common good of a society is both an ideal and a real goal, rather than distorted by conditions whereby only those in the most advantaged social classes have access to opportunities, resources, and rewards.

The inequalities that inevitably result from the existence of different social classes must be tempered, as much as possible, by achieving widespread access to opportunities to change social class positions. Societies need avenues of social mobility built into their social classes, so that there are sufficient opportunities to achieve personal goals within the common good. We cannot afford to let our social classes become castes, which prevent both upward and downward mobility. Rather, societies need social classes which are sufficiently flexible in their boundaries and opportunity structures to allow movement in both directions.

Social stratification is a historical fact, in that all settled societies have had some kind of social classes, even though the bases of classes have varied greatly through time. Because social classes have been present in all societies, it is difficult to discern alternative ways of organizing populations. However, this does not mean that social classes are inevitable, or that because we share a long history of social classes, they are necessary for future societies.

One of the legacies of having social classes is that divisions of labor are often directly linked to particular social stratification systems, such as colonial domination and slavery, or lifetime caste designations to perform specific tasks. An important goal of social intelligence, which aims to increase social justice, is working toward dissociating social classes from specific labor obligations or labor expectations.

III. Families and Social Class

Another concern in understanding the impact of social classes on families is not only to recognize the significance of distributions of power within societies, but also to take into account the distributions of power within social classes in the international community. Global stratification assumes increasing importance, because of the growing power of our single global economy, with its increasingly specialized divisions of labor among countries, and the power of multinational corporations over labor migrations among countries. Consequently, social classes are not only internal to particular societies, but also global in their outreach and influences on families.

For the purposes of *Families and Social Intelligence*, one of the most meaningful starting points to understand relationships between families and social classes is to examine the shared experiences of families and social classes in particular societies. Questions are asked later about how social intelligence can guide families and social classes in globalization processes, especially because many family members migrate more freely than ever before, in order to find interesting and well-paid jobs to support themselves and their families.

Caste and Mobility

The most ancient way that people organized their families and communities was to divide families and communities into groups according to sex and age. Our evolutionary development shows that this social organization within families, clans, and communities is one of the very earliest, enduring social structures. Thus divisions of labor among family members were originally based on the two criteria of sex and age, and family members' roles were defined for a lifetime by families' and communities' expectations for people of different sexes and different ages.

Thus, the largest, most essential parts of family members' lives were historically defined by sex and age social class categories, and their day-to-day behavior tended to conform to sex and age expectations that had been passed down from generation to generation. In some cases, perhaps with just a few cultural modifications, these same sex and age social classes persist in present day societies or communities, especially in agricultural and rural settings.

Recorded historical examples of sex and age expectations within families show us that the social outcomes for family members were virtually synonymous with living within caste systems. There was, and sometimes still is in the present, very little or no social mobility—with regard to sex and age—within or between generations. Because family members inherit their sex and age when they are born, the social and emotional systems of family cultures were experienced as immovable forces by family members. Fatalistic thinking frequently permeated world views in the past, due to the fact that sex and age social classes essentially determined personal and social destinies.

Social intelligence is a tool that helps us to understand the social roots from whence we came, and to see what options we have today in relation to our social origins. The fact that caste-like social structures, based on criteria of sex and age, existed in the longest histories of our families does not mean that this structure will inevitably exist in the present. Rather, we need to be alert to and aware of the extent of prolonged influences or institutionalization that these earliest forms of families and social classes still have in contemporary families. Sex and age social classes—or their rudiments—exist in many societies today, and even our most modern families, when stressed, frequently return to these former patterns of family interaction. Social intelligence makes us aware that, given this history, it is beneficial to create freer exchanges among family members, so that there can be both more openness in our families, and more social mobility within and between generations.

Entrapment in unchanging family structures is a serious problem, which affects entire families, as well as their individual members. The most visible patterns of family interaction, which resemble caste formations, are those that are organized on bases of historical or traditional sex and gender roles, as well as on bases of historical or traditional age roles. Rigidity in these sex and age social classes creates castes with little or no social mobility for family members.

In reality the wide range of variability among families reflects degrees of caste and degrees of social mobility for most family members, rather than the extremes of rigid castes with no mobility and completely open social class mobility. However, it is not widely known, or appreciated, that sex and age traditions become family limits on our freedom, which are still powerful and compelling. As a consequence, social influences that seem to facilitate the survival of families and clans, may actually work against the individual interests of many family or clan members.

In reviewing the social conditions that exist within families, particularly in one's own family, it is important to notice the extent to which castes and lack of mobility exist in our everyday family exchanges. Sometimes the banality of ongoing family interactions obfuscates caste and mobility issues in our families. However, social intelligence helps us to be more aware of what our real interests are, and what our options are, with regard to bringing about changes in family situations that are particularly relentless or unyielding in their restrictiveness.

Social classes based on sex and age are easier to observe, and link to caste and mobility, than social classes based on other dimensions of social exchanges or social values. Sex and age are highly visible characteristics that are shared by all human beings. However, degrees of caste and mobility in our families are also related to criteria such as economic means, educational achievement, race, ethnicity, and able-bodiedness.

The first two of these categories—economic means and educational achievement—are characteristically so fluid, for example, that shifts in patterns of family interaction can occur around these two issues in relatively short periods of time. Getting a well-paid job, inheriting resources from a relative, or graduating with a professional degree are special events or turning points that have substantial social class impacts on our everyday family exchanges and behavior. By contrast, social class bases such as race, ethnicity, and able-bodiedness—because they are often rooted in largely unchangeable physiological differences—tend to support caste-like exchanges among family members, as well as restricted social class mobility in societies. For example, some families express caste-like patterns of interaction, which both reflect and reinforce lacks of mobility in societies.

Because family attitudes and behaviors which create castes and limit mobility are learned, these patterns of interaction can be changed. However, the emotional intensity of most families often makes this likelihood remote, especially because many of our advantages and privileges depend on the entrapment or limitations of others, including members of our families. Social intelligence sheds light on these tendencies and complexities, and suggests that we pursue social class ideals that will ultimately increase social justice. When we use social intelligence to guide our behavior, we work more effectively toward reducing castes in our families, as well as toward increasing mobility or freedom within generations, between generations, and in societies.

Division of Labor

Families' social classes and social classes in societies meet important stabilizing needs, like maintaining continuities in how families and societies are organized through time. This mutual reinforcement between families and social classes has perpetuated stratification systems throughout history. Another important task, that social class divisions accomplish, is to serve as foundations for widely recognized divisions of labor. For example, India's caste system reflects a particular division of labor, which is based on beliefs in the sacred duties of caste members to perform different kinds of work.

One advantage of having specific links between social classes and divisions of labor is that this is a relatively clear-cut means of knowing who is going to do what in everyday life. Social classes were fairly well demarcated in the past, and widely-held assumptions about the work people in certain social classes would do were both realistic and predictable. This stability in social organization eased needs for extensive patterns of communication, as long as particular individuals or groups did not demand better conditions for themselves.

The broad parameters of social classes and divisions of labor have been stable and relatively unchanged for centuries in some societies, and remnants of this rudimentary social organization persist in today's modern societies. However, divisions of labor in families, as well as in societies, vary increasingly because social classes are now defined by educational achievement, gender and sexual orientation, race, ethnicity, and able-bodiedness as well as economic means. Social classes continue to be strong determinants of occupational choice, and options are limited or expanded according to the ways in which social classes are defined.

Links between social classes and divisions of labor affect families directly. For example, privileged work, where tasks performed in favorable work conditions receive the greatest rewards, is consistently easier for people from more prestigious social classes to attain. These work privileges provide further benefits for their middle or upper class family members. By contrast, when a person is born into a family of low social class, it is more or less predictable that the occupational opportunities and work available to these family members will have less desirable conditions, tasks, and rewards.

Divisions of labor within families tend to reflect social class influences, with people of different genders often having contrasting sets of expectations. For example, in nuclear families where family income may appear to be more or less equally earned among family members, men and women are usually assigned different tasks, frequently with women assuming more demanding and more time-consuming work responsibilities for family well-being than men. Statistical trends show that women continue to labor in the home more than men, even in two-career families, while at the same time most women are paid less for their work out of the home than men, and have less access to families' shared resources.

Families and Social Intelligence

From the point of view of social intelligence and family divisions of labor, the question must be asked how families can become freer for all their family members. Is it possible to organize family tasks so that there is more fluidity in dividing onerous, less pleasant responsibilities, especially where domestic chores and child care are concerned? If there is no agreement between spouses or parents about sharing these tasks more equitably, how can one family member—usually the person who is most stressed by present arrangements—bring about changes which decrease tensions and promote social justice?

Ideally families and social classes do not suffer from division of labor arrangements. When parents are dissatisfied with their present in-family child care arrangements, for example, they make changes in their daily routines, if only so that they can become stronger positive examples for their children. Without this kind of questioning and deliberate interruption of day-to-day responsibilities, ongoing behavior will reinforce families' unsatisfactory but repeated divisions of labor, which cannot meet contemporary family, individual, or social needs.

Family members need to be wary and watchful about families' tendencies to develop overly rigid divisions of labor. Static divisions of labor within families are difficult to change when we concentrate only on the specific ways that labor is divided. Attention should be paid to some of the links between social class and family divisions of labor, in order to understand underlying social inequalities, if we are to create healthier and more meaningful divisions of labor within families.

Tackling problems of inequality in families need not threaten family stability in the long run, even though there will be some temporary instability because of necessary readjustments. Having a more flexible division of labor, particularly where responsibilities for certain tasks are shared or swapped, can go a long way to breaking down the relentless rigidity which permeates family divisions of labor that are traditional, or automatically taken for granted. Social justice in families' divisions of labor may be attained, to some extent, merely by moving in directions which yield new kinds of more egalitarian adaptations.

Power

Power is closely associated with social classes, whatever bases the hierarchies of social classes have. For example, power is wielded by those in the upper classes of the varied hierarchies. Power also creates gaps between the haves and the have-nots in societies: the haves wield most of the power, so that those who have the most assets frequently exploit the relatively powerless have-nots.

Power is omnipresent, at least potentially, in social relationships, patterns of interaction, families, groups, organizations, communities, and societies. Power is the capacity to coerce individuals and collectivities to act in ways which are not necessarily in their own self interest. We are particularly vulnerable to the domination of others because we are social beings. Our needs for each other, in order to survive, make any exploitation of this neediness a constant danger.

Families are caught up in webs of domination which derive from emotional systems, beliefs, varied social classes, cultures, and societies. When we examine patterns of interaction within families, as well as patterns of social influences on families, we begin to see where power lies in given situations. This is no trivial task. However, optimally we should know the power relations in our everyday routines and situations, as well as how vulnerable we are to others' pressures, and how we can change some of these imbalances. One effective strategy for neutralizing, or even leveling, the distribution of power in our families is to define the injustices we see in particular settings, and to move in directions that increase social justice. Sometimes this involves participating in collective actions to reduce the negative and harmful effects of imbalanced power relations.

To some extent it is useful to have a zero-sum concept of power in mind when trying to understand power distributions within families and in societies. This means that those who have power necessarily leave others without power, because the power in any given situation—latent, dormant, or activated—is limited. Because we are usually not in positions where we can generate sufficient power as needed, we need to understand how power is connected to particular statuses, jobs, and social situations, in order to maintain a sufficient degree of control over our lives.

When we consider families in society, their commonly shared lack of direct representation in political processes makes us aware that although most people give lip service to the importance of families to societies, many families are made up of relatively powerless people, who cannot easily act in their own interests. Families may be exploited easily by employers or religious groups, for example, and some families gradually fall apart because there are insufficient community supports.

The weakness and vulnerability of many families is important to acknowledge in understanding why families have to deal with so many stresses and tensions. Power relations in the broader social contexts of families, including international dynamics, frequently deprive families or family members of opportunities to express and represent their own interests. Consequently, unless families can be guided by social intelligence, or can receive sufficient direct care and attention, they may easily break down.

Many family crises in modern day societies result from the rapid social changes of the twentieth and twenty-first centuries. For example, the economic and political powers that derive from capitalism and large corporate profits have infiltrated our daily lives. Economic market influences often dominate our ways of thinking, being, and doing because, as families and societies, we have not yet learned how to withstand constant commercial pressures.

Whatever the particular economic and social influences are on our families and societies, modernization has brought dramatic religious and secular changes. Power relations in our cultures now permeate personal aspects of family life: romantic love, sex, gender, sexual orientation, age differences, childbirth, parenting, marriage, and divorce. Mass media manipulate and exploit human nature, as well as individual or collective dreams. As a consequence, we tend to feel relatively powerless in relation to the overwhelming strength of media influences in the complex and significant spheres of work, advertising, lifestyles, and leisure pursuits.

This kind of subtle economic and political power reaches into our souls. If we remain passive in today's modern society, we become increasingly powerless and increasingly vulnerable to power takeovers in our political systems. In contrast to these debilitating changes, social intelligence is a tool to empower us, a way to protect our families, and a means whereby we stay alert to the patterns of power in our lives. Optimally social intelligence guides us and our families to lead more meaningful lives, as well as to increase the common good for all.

Economic Resources and Education

The most universal criterion used to define social classes in both historical and modern societies is economic resources. Societies use money, in its many different forms, as a meaningful way to make status distinctions, and to demarcate social classes among individuals and families. This criterion of social class divisions is crucial for families, in that economic resources are essential for both survival and fulfillment. Thus, although accumulating finances may not be an ideal or goal in its own right, financial assets are consistently the most reliable means to achieve a wide range of preferred goals.

Economic assets are not only necessary to cover the continuing basic needs of families and individuals, but they are also important in providing security and protection from hazards in the present and future. The fact that families possess sufficient or surplus economic means enables them to participate in a wide variety of activities, and to share more of the rewards that society has to offer. We make financial investments in our futures, and in the future of our offspring, by giving financial help to members of younger generations of our families, and by transmitting accumulated assets to them when we die.

To the extent that these uses of economic resources by family members give them social advantages, social mobility becomes more assured than if these families did not have sufficient economic resources. We essentially create our own social mobility when we have access to more than adequate economic means to meet our basic needs. Economic resources can therefore reduce many—although not all—of the coercive aspects of social classes, and we become relatively free of the caste-like characteristics of social classes through the ways we choose to spend our adequate financial resources.

One of the most significant items which families purchase for their children is a good education, especially higher education, given the emphasis on credentials in modern societies. Even though some educational facilities are available to family members free of charge, or at minimal costs, there are numerous ways in which economic assets make crucial differences in determining educational outcomes for children and young adults in families which have surplus economic resources. It is humbling to consider that our current social standing may be more due to the educational expenses paid by our parents and family members, as well as to their emotional support, than to our own efforts to learn.

In the total scheme of things, education may become a more effective avenue of social mobility for individuals than economic means alone. Thus, how we spend our money often pays off. Buying endless toys and baubles, including adult amusements and leisure activities, will not yield the rich dividends that education, or perhaps travel abroad, will predictably bring. Education for life is a serious and strenuous matter, which frequently costs a great deal of money, especially when adult family members assume responsibilities not only for themselves, but also for their children and grandchildren.

Social intelligence, which includes being aware of different social class dynamics, as well as the influences of social strains toward upward and downward social mobility, enables us to weigh some of the pros and cons of economic resources and education. When we understand that being trapped by social classes, whatever their organizing principles, is harmful to us and our families, we begin to see more options and ways to create meaningful avenues of mobility, if only to claim freedom from some of our social class restraints. We need to understand not only how social classes work, but also how to change their forceful impacts and stresses.

Economic resources and education are not only important in their own right, but they also influence allocations of tasks and distributions of power within families. Economic assets are frequently a determining factor in both divisions of labor—usually through educational achievements—and distributions of power in families. In some families the readiness to marry, for example, may be determined by individual family members' accumulations of resources, which are equated with being mature. However, it is difficult to accumulate sufficient economic resources to be independent and self sufficient in today's societies, because these usually depend directly on our paid work, as well as on our educational attainments.

The impact of gender and sexual orientation in social classes can be somewhat neutralized by our families' economic resources and education. Having sufficient finances protects and enables us to articulate what it is that we need, and what it is that we should change in our daily routines in order to live more freely. Similarly the negative consequences that flow from social classes based on race and ethnicity can be neutralized to some extent by having adequate economic resources and advanced education. It is not that money can buy anything, but rather that social intelligence can guide us to use our money to buy effective strategies to combat the coercive powers of those social class restraints that limit our lives the most.

Gender and Sexual Orientation

Families are important because they transmit knowledge about personal definitions of gender and sexual orientation to members of the youngest generations. The earliest stages of our social development are more influential in building our social awareness than later stages of development, however deliberate and self-conscious we become in building our own identities and characters. In fact, many of our hard-earned efforts to change ourselves are aimed at undoing our earliest socialization, and at trying to re-socialize ourselves in ways that are more meaningful or more realistic.

It is helpful to think of gender and sexual orientation as significant social classes, because many public reactions to gender and sexual orientation objectify and pigeon-hole us in others' categories. By deliberately considering gender and sexual orientation as social classes, we move away from being stigmatized or victimized by others, toward taking charge of our own definitions of ourselves. Even though gender and sexual orientation are personal rather than family issues, these aspects of our being have important family and social class dimensions.

Families have their own sets of usually well-demarcated gender and sexual orientation expectations for their children. In most families, unless there have already been deviations from average gender and sexual orientations in previous generations, members' expectations for their children tend to follow broad societal norms for gender and sexual orientations, in part depending on their economic resources and social class positions. For example, some leeway is often given for gender and sexual orientations in the wealthiest classes, because difficult-to-deal-with facts are disguised more easily by surplus economic resources. By contrast, children in middle and lower economic class families may be held to more rigid gender and sexual orientation standards, partly in order to present to others what is considered to be conventional, or the same as most families in that society.

Gender social classes in many families have historically shown patterns of behavior that not only went along with whatever contemporary norms were, but also tended to have backward-looking biases. For example, gender traditions very clearly distinguished what is feminine from what is masculine, and these standards still permeate many current concerns about family respectability. Only when education for women was deemed appropriate, in the twentieth century, were increased numbers of women able to pursue learning to become economically and socially independent. Until then, both women and men were subject to caste-like social relations, where there were relatively few overlapping experiences or interests between men and women, and where historical, traditional norms held sway in their personal relationships.

More recently social concerns have shifted from thinking about gender as a simple dichotomy, to considering the many variants of sexual orientation. Given the fact that male and female genders have been long-time bases of social classes, where historically men subordinated women through a caste-like hierarchy, there is now a more complex and a more volitional hierarchy of gender and sexual orientation definitions, especially because of the relatively recent importance given to gender and sexual orientations in both private and public settings. This surge of social change includes heterosexuality and homosexuality as sometimes contested bases of sexual orientation, with heterosexuality usually being more predominant, due to mainstream societies' traditions and customs.

Because many people believe that sexual orientation is innate rather than chosen, however, categories of sexual orientation may also assume their own caste-like dimensions. Not only do men and women form social classes, which cannot easily be substituted for each other, and which do not allow much mobility from one social class of gender to the other, but sexual orientation classes also make social hierarchies more complex and more caste-like.

Individual families and individual family members frequently follow precedents established by societies, in order to unsnarl their particular gender and sexual orientation issues, because many individuals and families do not yet know how to deal effectively with these concerns. However, the more social intelligence guides family interactions, and the more gender and sexual orientations are thought of as social classes, the more successful family adaptations can be.

Economic means, educational achievement, race, ethnicity, and able-bodiedness are other social class dimensions which affect families' reactions to gender and sexual orientation. Having more economic means and higher levels of educational attainment, for example, can help families to formulate thoughtful adaptations and options for their gender and sexual orientation issues. Social intelligence guides families to cope with variations in norms around gender and sexual orientation, as well as related race, ethnicity, and able-bodied concerns.

Race and Ethnicity

Race and ethnicity play different roles in different societies and different families, and are related but different bases of social classes. Even when race and ethnicity are integrally connected, they have distinctive characteristics which are somewhat separate. Race, for example, is usually more visually evident than ethnicity, so that like gender, race is a relatively easy way for populations to divide themselves into social classes. When this happens, the negative consequences of social classes—based on either race or gender—strongly resemble relatively static castes. Whether race and gender are considered in relation to societies or families, their caste-like dimensions are more easily identified than those of ethnicity.

Ethnicity may also have some visual characteristics that serve as a base for social classes, although this base may be broader and more cultural in substance than the social class base of race. Like gender, ethnicity has complex values, beliefs, and lifestyles that define ethnic hierarchies, and reflect degrees of social acceptance in the broader society. These more inclusive qualities do not remove the caste characteristics of ethnicity in some social settings, but the caste characteristics of ethnicity are usually less visibly marked than those of race and gender.

When race and ethnicity are social classes, they frequently evoke prejudice and discrimination, possibly to the extremes of violence or warfare. Social intelligence requires that we come to terms with our actual or latent hatreds, so that we use our passions more constructively to increase social justice. We should continuously ask ourselves to what extent the established powers in society use racism to establish biased standards to serve their own individual or family interests. Also, to what extent do patterns in our own family interactions result from racist forces in the wider society? How can we avoid perpetuating racism and ethnic intolerance in our families, so that the youngest generations build more just worlds for the future?

One of the ways in which racism and ethnic intolerance are assessed in our own families is to observe how our families treat racial and ethnic minorities. When our family members marry—or choose people from other races or ethnic groups as friends and dates—how do our family members respond? To what extent does trying to absorb people from different races or ethnic groups into our families upset our relatives' usual ways of doing things, and challenge those who hold the most power in our families?

In order to design strategies to live more freely with race and ethnicity, we must see social class divisions as artificial human inventions that are riddled with flaws and errors. Responsibilities to put right some of the wrongs of the past, with regard to race and ethnicity, are onerous. It is easy to be discouraged, especially when we realize that dedicating our lives to achieving such ideals may not make much difference in the total scheme of things in our societies today. However, if we go about our daily business with this goal clearly in mind, as well as act deliberately to accomplish social justice whenever possible, societies will gradually increase the social freedom of all races and ethnic groups. Furthermore, these goals can be more easily accomplished, to a limited extent, in our own families.

Race and ethnicity vary in their impacts on and within families, depending on particular races and ethnicities, as well as on their specific societies. Sometimes it is useful to consider how religions uphold or neutralize social class differences of race and ethnicity, and to see how economic assets and educational achievements reduce some of the caste-like qualities of these social classes. Divisions of labor evolve from race and ethnic differences, as well as from power differences, while at the same time gender, sexual orientation, and able-bodiedness affect the social classes of races and ethnic groups.

Even though the overlapping bases of racial and ethnic social classes are complex and difficult to understand, social intelligence guides us to use enlightened strategies to deal with them. When we are more aware of the importance and complexity of race and ethnicity in our collective survival and fulfillment, for example, we become more deliberate and more effective in our behavior, and work more competently with others to improve our worlds.

IV. Families and Culture

F amilies and culture are strongly related, although we often do not realize or acknowledge this. In many respects the power of culture works in unobtrusive ways—by influencing what we take for granted. However, culture is a social reality which needs to be reckoned with, and we cannot afford to let culture define our perceptions and behavior without raising serious questions about its social sources.

Not only do social class cultures help to maintain social class differences in our societies, but also the content of our mainstream cultures—beliefs, values, ideals, laws, expectations, norms, standards, images, symbols, meaning, and knowledge—is saturated with ideas and ideals about families. These cultural representations of families have powerful influences on what we notice in our everyday lives, how we think, and what we do. Even our deepest levels of consciousness are strongly affected by cultural ideas and ideals: for example, we dream in cultural terms.

The social institutions of society—family, religion, the economy, education, and political systems—are founded on basic values and beliefs of our cultures, as well as on values and beliefs about families. Thus we cannot go far in our day-to-day lives without drawing upon different aspects of our cultures. Social intelligence leads us to appreciate the extent to which there are many diverse cultures in our societies, some of these being more publicly recognizable and more acknowledged than others. Social intelligence also helps us to see the more widely shared national and international cultures, which make communications and exchanges within and among societies possible.

One of the most important aspects of these intercultural dynamics is the extent to which mainstream cultures represent whole societies. If only one, or very few, social classes are reflected in a particular mainstream culture, for example, this society is dominated by specific interest groups. If many social classes are absorbed into a mainstream culture, or coexist with the mainstream culture in readily apparent ways, this is a more diverse and democratic society.

Modernization, secularization, and recent social changes have brought varied cultures into being, which are more democratic than was possible when small, isolated societies perpetuated themselves according to traditions and precedents. A single culture is more dominant in small traditional societies, while many different high—or sophisticated—cultures, as well as popular cultures, are found in contemporary mass societies. In modern societies high cultures usually represent the dominant interests and leisure pursuits of upper social classes or elites, and often require or assume higher levels of educational attainment by their participants than popular cultures.

Most cultures are saturated with imagery and symbolism about families and personal relationships. Although this content may be directed toward the consumption patterns and needs of particular social classes, the family and relationship images of cultures' pervasive symbols are inescapable. Living in today's societies makes us vulnerable to contemporary cultural patterns and changes. For example, the social impacts of our latest fads and fashions show us how strongly we want to conform to changing standards as they change. This impetus is also found in other social activities: fads and fashions influence spending patterns, political goals and strategies, educational programs, religious expressions, reproduction rates, expressions of sexualities, and gender styles.

Modern cultures are significant adaptations that enhance societies' survival and fulfillment, and they need to be understood for the powerful influences they have on family relations and family well-being. Modern cultures sometimes oppose traditions of the past, especially where traditions have continued to be influential in contemporary societies. However, modern cultures do not necessarily radically change or reform traditions, even though some past-oriented traditions may have what appear to be harmful social effects in the present. Overall, culture is an established way to innovate in society, which may offer beacons of possibilities for both immediate and far-off futures.

Laws are essential parts of modern cultures. Pivotal legislation—such as no-fault divorce or the decriminalization of abortion—shows how institutionalized value changes can have major consequences for families and societies. However, because laws can be reversed, the increased choices and freedoms achieved through legal changes may be temporary.

Social intelligence enables us to see the many ways in which cultural changes affect the well-being of societies, and contribute to the adaptations that we make as societies change. Social intelligence guides us in designing cultural changes—individually and collectively—and helps us to strengthen particular values in our families and societies. For example, values such as equality, inclusiveness, diversity, cooperation, and openness cannot be assumed to exist in modern democracies. Rather we must re-forge these values at every opportunity, by making commitments and working toward increasing social justice.

Culture Today

In order to gain socially intelligent perspectives on our cultures today, we need to consider the cultural contrasts that have emerged in time, through questioning what the growth of civilization, democracy, modernization, and secularization have meant for our present-day cultures and societies. We also need to know the extent to which the breakdown of local communities, in today's modern societies, has resulted in a lessening of cultural influences.

The cultures of contemporary industrial societies are complex and multifaceted, whereas past cultures were more or less homogeneous. Our current heterogeneous cultures represent mosaics of racial and ethnic diversity, as well as overlapping social classes. However, mainstream cultural cores of societies often produce and sustain patterns of institutional behavior, because they represent the most powerful groups' values, beliefs, ideas, ideals, and expectations.

The changing dimensions of culture show that our societies have become more diverse. Culture has either adapted to, or been in the vanguard of these changes by including increased differences in values, beliefs, and ideals. These broad cultural influences have direct impacts on our families, so that alongside the traditional families that still exist in modern societies, we see many varied families. The variant family forms and processes found in modern societies result in part from differences in social classes, races, ethnicities, nuclear families, extended kin, single-parent families, and gay families.

Alongside changes in the public's acceptance of a wide variety of families in societies are increases in freedom within and among families. Although modern day families and societies are neither disorganized nor liberal, when we compare them with expectations at the beginning of the twentieth century, we see that the iron grip of traditional cultural standards in the conduct of everyday family life and societies has been considerably loosened.

Given this significant shift in family and societal cultures in the last century, today's cultural standards appear to some as too permissive, or as moving in destructive directions. However, although the social consequences and implications of all cultural changes are extremely significant for families, cultures today are perhaps more accurately thought of as complex masses of diverse social changes. Our cultures do not aim expressly to modify family patterns, for example. Rather, they are collective efforts to adapt to changing ideas and shifting circumstances. In this context, families and family cultures are merely integral parts of vast ongoing changes.

IV. Families and Culture

Today's societies necessarily deal with situations that have not been encountered before. Our increasingly complex cultures do not provide clear-cut guidance, standards, or expectations to families as they did a century ago. By contrast, the diverse cultures which flourish in today's industrial societies offer a wide range of options and possibilities for individual and family being and doing, which are not yet clear or obvious. Social intelligence is a valuable tool for clarifying our choices, given the complexity of today's cultures, because it can direct or suggest ways for individuals and families to proceed. Social intelligence simplifies the myriad choices that exist, and points out some of the more meaningful options within contemporary cultures.

Our modern cultures may not need to be changed radically when families' members make more constructive life choices, or work toward resolving social justice issues for all families. Even though concerted efforts are necessarily called for to change those aspects of our cultures which affect many families negatively, we must give primacy to making our own appropriate choices for our actions today, as well as to our families' well-being.

Cultures in most modern industrial societies allow considerable freedom within families, with the result that many contemporary family members are robust, strong, and independent. When we encourage families to support the autonomy of all their members, as well as to help family members to understand the complexities of their emotional relationship systems, we contribute positively toward realizing important societal goals.

Social intelligence helps us to get our priorities in line, so that we do not succumb to temptations and distractions from our current cultures. Furthermore, social intelligence anchors our decisions and behavior, so that we choose not to waste our time and energies, as though we have no responsibilities to our families, or to those who are less fortunate than ourselves.

One way to improve our families, through our existing cultures, is to learn as much as we can about those social conditions which have the strongest impact on our families. For example, we can use our awareness of cultural opportunities to take advantage of existing cultural means that will enhance our education, prepare us for meaningful work in society, and help us to articulate social goals that will increase the common good for all. Our present-day cultures are extremely powerful social and emotional systems that can be used either for the betterment of societies, or for their destruction. We consistently benefit from pausing in our daily routines, so that we gain sufficient time to formulate broad perspectives on the options we have to construct and implement positive social goals for the future. Social intelligence enlightens the decisions we and our families make as we move in these new directions.

Culture and Traditions

In the earliest societies, as well as in some contemporary rural or agricultural societies, culture and tradition overlap so much that they are virtually synonymous. In the distant past most families followed local traditions unquestioningly—in all aspects of their relationships, tasks, and responsibilities—from generation to generation. This cultural dominance of traditions meant that solutions to family problems derived mainly from local community ways of doing things, and that the repeated traditional definitions of families and individual responsibilities did not create significant conflicts. In fact, it was widely believed that family traditions caused social stability and community harmony.

Another characteristic of our earliest traditional families is that these families and their members were not yet aware of alternative ways of doing things. Rather they were in awe of the particular family traditions they knew, which seemed to hold mystical powers because they were believed to have existed from the beginning of time—or from eras before the childhood memories of their oldest family members.

One of the particular powers and mystical elements of tradition was, and still continues to be, the religious endorsement and support that traditions receive in many communities and societies. In part it is believed that some family traditions became established because of religious beliefs, rather than that religions developed through family or community traditions. Whatever the historical origins of traditions and religions, religious sanctions—together with family and community sanctions—make traditions a very powerful influence on families and their individual members.

In present-day societies, due to the complex processes of both secularization and modernization, some cultures seem to stand apart from mainstream values and beliefs, separating themselves from traditions and their supporting religious practices. Cultures which are independent of traditions and religions have increasingly developed, so that they now reflect the value priorities and preferences of many different groups of people. Sometimes alternative cultures, such as youth cultures, oppose mainstream values and beliefs, thus serving as beacons for or reflections of broad social changes. When societies need new visions in order to reorganize their priorities, the cultural detachment and objectivity of the values of alternative groups, such as peace movements, can have constructive impacts on whole societies. Also, resuscitated cultural values, such as equality, sometimes prove themselves essential for shedding new light on old problems.

Families are inevitably caught up in this maelstrom of cultural changes. Traditions, with their religious supports, perpetuate themselves into the present, and co-exist with new cultural forms. As a result of these cultural shifts, families develop a wide range of variations among themselves, as well as a wide range of different authorities to reinforce and justify their existence.

Even though families are not necessarily supported by either religions or traditions, they meet such fundamental needs in society that they seem to be relatively conservative influences in their own right. The fact that families have existed longer than societies suggests that some families have found valuable answers to the constant trials and tribulations of modern times. Social intelligence shows us that families throughout the world suffer from considerable social strains and pressures, and that new ways to sustain families need to be developed to enable them to meet their vital responsibilities for today's societies.

The rapid growth of capitalism has brought market forces to the fore in our current thinking and understanding about the relationship between cultures and traditions. Some erosion of sacredness in families followed in the wake of discoveries in modern technology, and the manufacture of higher standards of living. However, because cultures are repositories for all social values and beliefs, it is perhaps more expedient for us to try to understand the complexities and constructive promises of cultural solutions—for families and societies—than to succumb to the dominance of major corporations and their economic and political concerns.

All kinds of traditions can be called upon to neutralize some of the power that political interests wield over our families and the global economy. Families' most resilient adaptive powers, for example, need to be replicated if we are to build the kinds of families, cultures, and societies that can withstand contemporary economic and political pressures.

Social intelligence helps us to be more objective in our understanding of the strong influences of our traditions and cultures on our families. Social intelligence shows us not only the historical dimensions of these influences, but also their tenacity and in-depth effects through time. When we look at particular family and social traditions, such as marriage, or particular cultural values, such as equality, we deepen our understanding of the symbolic and practical meanings of our families.

Social intelligence suggests ways to make changes that will strengthen our families. If we can design alternative groups that can meet wide ranges of our family needs, for example, we should do so. However, we can also discover new ways to support our families as they exist now, especially because most people do not want to radically change their existing families. When we focus on social intelligence and social justice, we ensure that we make constructive rather than destructive moves to strengthen our families.

Family Cultures

Families develop their own cultures, which are sometimes quite separate and distinct from cultures in societies. Even though the values, ideals, beliefs, and expectations of family cultures are drawn from mainstream cultures, and from different social class cultures within mainstream cultures, there is much latitude for families to create their own combinations of beliefs and values as family cultures. In fact, sometimes family cultures become so unique in their own right that they essentially challenge the beliefs and values of mainstream societies, or they represent innovative alternatives to other family cultures in a given society.

The strength of many individuals derives directly from their own family cultures. Although we often look to societies for precedents of how to act, and of which choices to make with regard to serious issues like our occupations, in the final analysis we are more likely to depend on our original family cultures for our ideals, motivations, values, and beliefs than on our societies. This happens partly through our own volition—we choose our family cultures as sources of our inspiration, because we believe that the values and beliefs of our family cultures are best for us—or because we are merely more familiar with the values and beliefs of our family cultures. When we become used to our family cultures, we automatically make them our own, even though optimally we should be more critical about accepting which values we own.

To some extent cultures exist in all families, as these are necessary for basic communications among family members. Family cultures do not merely replicate societal cultures, but rather have their own patterns of give and take, depending on the values and needs of different family members. It is especially families and their kin groups, which stay meaningfully in touch with each other, that articulate the most distinctive family cultures. Ideally we make family communications with relatives from different generations in order to enrich our family cultures. To the extent that all family members contribute to a given family culture, the specific values and beliefs of that family culture are both inclusive and flexible.

In the absence of this kind of freedom in constructing family cultures, a few family members usually dominate weaker family members, as well as members of younger generations, by insisting that their own particular values and beliefs are accepted by all. This dynamic sets up autocratic rather than democratic family relationships, where most family members sacrifice their rights to choose values and beliefs for themselves, and the dominant few practice their preferences. The fundamentalist family cultures that result from these influences are rigid, dogmatic, and bigoted. They lack a healthy, life-enhancing breadth of vision, and they do not nurture the priority of autonomy for all family members.

Establishing freedom and autonomy in family cultures is very significant. The assumptions we make, and the values we hold about self and others, are both evident in and basic to our family cultures. Social intelligence helps us to become aware of significant patterns of dependency and unofficial rule in our family cultures, and shows us how to make essential or meaningful modifications of these patterns when needed. In order to see these relationship and dependency issues, we must be as objective as possible about who is doing what in our families, and how this is supported by our family cultures of beliefs, values, ideals, and expectations.

These characteristics and options of family cultures show that the particular beliefs, values, and ideals in our families are closely tied to their power structures. Family cultures do not operate in a vacuum. They have distinct power dimensions which need to be examined, rather than ignored, if family freedom is to be created or maintained. Our families' power dimensions are also intimately associated with issues such as whether or not to change family cultures, and how to change family cultures. Even though broad external cultural influences, like modernization and secularization, inevitably influence our family cultures, families retain considerable autonomy for themselves through their individual members, and through their degrees of family integration.

Family cultures are increasingly influenced by mass media images of families. However, there is usually a cultural lag in the content of mass media communications and representations, in that most modern family forms shown by the media are not taken as seriously as traditional families. Nevertheless, social intelligence suggests that media influences on family cultures will increase in the future, and will have significant consequences for family cultures in globalization.

Culture and Power

Culture is a force in its own right, so it can be thought of as having power, or even as being power. Wherever there is sufficient agreement about beliefs and values—for example, in beliefs and values about families—this particular strand of public opinion can be a strong influence throughout society. A high level of consensus about traditions, especially ways to conduct family relations, can establish long-lasting trends throughout societies, as well as among countries with similar industrial development, races, or ethnicities.

Cultures also have their own elites who wield power. For example, the lifestyles of so-called successful members in societies influence how others in these societies run their lives, and what they want to achieve. Cultures set standards for societies to follow, and these influence patterns of interaction beyond the individuals concerned: cultures lead fashions, art forms, research goals, and ways of thinking.

Families' cultures form both independently and in relation to societies' cultures. Because both family cultures and societies' more external cultures influence what we do, each of these cultures has power over us, often in ways which we do not realize. Also, we frequently need to remind ourselves that we are human only because we have absorbed particular values and beliefs from cultural sources. Our very being is a cultural product, so that who we are and what we do are influenced not only by our cultural choices, but also by the cultures from which we choose.

If we have particular family problems, social intelligence shows us that it is beneficial to consider these issues in light of our most significant cultural influences. When we recognize and respect the power of cultures, we make saner choices among our values and beliefs. If necessary, for example, we immerse ourselves in alternative cultures, in order to have new or different sources of values and beliefs from which to draw. Cultures are consistently meaningful and powerful sources of interpersonal and societal changes, so that cultures can inspire new visions of what is possible in our families and in societies.

Education is a cultural means of understanding our environments and resources. In most societies knowledge is power, and we increase our cultural power when we learn something. For example, getting into habits of learning as much as we can about the world gives us a constant supply of knowledge beyond our formal academic learning, which provides us with power, or at least a degree of control, over our circumstances.

Accumulating power in society, through economic resources and political strategies, is predictably achieved by fostering particular beliefs and strategies. Many dictators and world leaders have access to vast economic and political resources, and these accumulations of wealth provide both power and cultures of power. Wealthy leaders often create rationales to maintain their privileges, and this vital cultural underpinning reinforces and increases material aspects of their dominance.

Because of the complex interrelations between culture and power, we need to understand the significance of family cultures, and the ways in which family cultures result from broader societal cultures and the international community. We need to understand how culture can be a source of enlightenment and inspiration, either in problem-solving, or in creating better conditions for our families and others. If we choose to advance the value of diversity, for example, how do we use family and societal cultures to accomplish this? Can the value of diversity gain sufficient power in our families to really influence our behavior? How can we continue to strengthen the cultural value of diversity, so that it transforms the ways we do things in our families and in societies?

We experience the power of culture directly through our choices, and by identifying with the particular values we want in our family cultures. When we deliberately select one or more values—such as diversity, inclusiveness, equality, cooperation, or openness—we can begin lifelong journeys to incorporate these values in our family cultures, societal cultures, and global cultures. Optimally, our chosen values gradually gain sufficient momentum to move us from idea to action. However, it is especially through our collective actions that the power of culture and the power of change become apparent, so that broader social realities can be rebuilt.

Changing Cultures

History shows us that cultures have made dramatic changes through time, and that we can characterize cultures as being more or less humane in their tolerance or support for particular kinds of behavior. Attitudes and actions in the same societies have varied considerably, for example, depending on the particular values espoused in both societal and family cultures. We became democratic societies through changing our cultures, and democracy has perpetuated itself because of widespread education in values which support democratic ideals.

Social intelligence helps us to understand the power and complexity of cultural changes, in all their variants, and guides us in introducing new kinds of cultural changes. We often accomplish broad social changes through changing our cultures, or make substantive changes in our patterns of family interaction through modifying our family cultures.

Considering the importance of families and family cultures includes recognizing the fluidity of the core beliefs, values, ideals, and knowledge that make up our cultures. Given the fact that culture is essentially a body of shared practices and standards, which have been socially formulated and learned, many different kinds of changes can be produced through our cultures. Our most significant human achievements often depend on the cultures we are born into, because these cultures are the sources of how we first became human.

In order to see some of the complexities in the overlapping layers of our cultures, we need to examine many of the different adaptations that individuals, families, and societies make to each other, especially during globalization. This helps us understand why cultural changes influence our families and societies. Even if we did very little throughout our lifetimes, for example, our cultures would continue to adapt to our passivity and inactivity. In these respects, our changing cultures are foundations of our existence and survival. However, we can also change the beliefs, values, and ideals that drive the cultural changes around us. We can increase social justice when we deliberately make different value choices, and when we apply social justice values in our everyday exchanges with others.

Realizing that what we learn allows us to see the world differently, as well as to act differently, suggests that our family and societal cultures are predisposed to change. Although there are limits to the kinds of changes that we can accomplish, we can at least make commitments to stay open to new possibilities, and to act accordingly.

Cultural change is a fact of life, and a primary characteristic of modern societies. Social intelligence is based on acknowledging these kinds of complex social and cultural realities. Furthermore, because we live in a world of physical and social consistencies, it is our shared responsibility to know as much as we can, as well as to do as much as we can, to improve our social and cultural conditions.

One of the circumstances we must deal with in changing our cultures is the resistance to change that we inevitably encounter. We need to develop strategies to overcome others' resistance, for example, so that we eventually move toward implementing those value choices and changes that we deem to be both right and appropriate. However, because of our innate interdependence, some degree of consensus in our families, or in societies, has to be attained in order to make these value changes.

Both internal and external resistances to our cultural initiatives are ongoing dynamics in our motivations, relationships, and social realities. This means that we have to be perceptive, as well as subtle, in how we pursue our ideals for creating a better world. Our families' patterns of resistance are usually more obvious than those in societies, for example, because of the greater frequency and intensity of emotions within families. The emotional volatility of our families suggests that social pressures for or against cultural changes can disrupt family relationships, or even eventually make our families extinct. Thus we have to be aware not only of the potential for changes in our family cultures, but also of their predictably strong resistance to change.

Social intelligence guides us through quagmires of social resistance, so that we can recognize attempts to sabotage our efforts to implement value changes in our families' and societies' cultures. When we take opportunities to nurture our ideals, we are more likely to successfully sustain our efforts to bring about cultural changes. By contrast, when we are passive, we are vulnerable to being swept along by major historical influences, such as modernization and secularization, which we may not want to perpetuate.

Modernization and Secularization

Given the power that broad social influences have to determine the quality of interaction in our families, the modernization and secularization of societal cultures have continuing impacts on our family cultures. Although modernization and secularization are sometimes thought of as being reciprocally related parts of the same complex social change processes, some distinctions can be drawn between them, especially with regard to how they affect family cultures and the importance of families in society.

Families and Social Intelligence

In many modern industrial societies, social changes in families and societies are customarily linked to the industrial revolution, modern technologies, and mass production. As material standards of living were raised through the development and refinement of market economies, families were increasingly concerned about their paid factory labor and their consumption of material goods. The economic developments of modernization changed our cultures, from valuing craft skills or goods to valuing profits, and from valuing people or relationships to valuing economic success. In addition, materialistic shifts in cultural values in wider societies infiltrated our families, and economic successes or failures between generations created upward social mobility or increased alienation.

Family members' historical preoccupations with survival and dignity were replaced by issues about how families can benefit from industrial production. Family members' education became a direct preparation for the market economy, rather than a transmission of knowledge for its own sake. Increased communications, through more efficient print and visual media, increased awareness of current events in societies, and allowed families to connect with groups beyond their local communities. Public opinion developed broader bases, and there was increased questioning of social class privileges both within and among families.

Some of this questioning by families raised religious issues. Heretofore families were supported by religious communities, and their members were educated within religions traditions. One way to be educated was to be religious, and one way to be religious was to learn appropriate religious texts. However, as the industrial revolution revealed a more connected, less mysterious world, there was a growing sense that perhaps religion did not answer all human questions. At the same time, the increasing economic power of profits through industrialization challenged religious beliefs and hierarchies that had been deeply entrenched for generations in many families.

IV. Families and Culture

Secularization resulted from a growth of diversity in the roles that religious believers and non-believers could play, and by increased awareness of the existence and importance of individuals and groups that did not hold religious beliefs. The stigma of being in a family which did not worship like other families was lessened, and increasing numbers of families developed world views which no longer gave primacy to religious interpretations of their everyday lives.

As secularization gathered momentum during industrialization, families not only questioned religion, but also discontinued many of the devotional practices of their elders. Although some families maintained their faith, and became more rigorous and more committed to their religions, modernization and secularization were accompanied by a greater overall acceptance of diversity in religious forms and practices.

Families have become both more secure and less secure in their inevitable absorption of some of these broad social influences of modernization and secularization. As new job openings and new work locations emerge, and economic success is experienced by at least some individuals and their families, values and possibilities change. Some families no longer thrive from holding on to their basic religious beliefs to explain this modern world. However, in losing the innocence of their religious faiths, families are also bereft of the much-needed assurances that religions bring, especially because societies are increasingly complex, and families must cope with increased conflicts of interest in order to survive and adapt. New cultures are therefore necessary to help families to support their members, and to enable them to leave home independently in order to lead honorable and productive lives.

Modernization and secularization usually involve travel and migrations to nearby cities or beyond. Young family members' travel breaks through the strict emotional controls of their older relatives, but at the same time these families may be fragmented by the increased numbers of nuclear families of parents and children that separate from their kin groups. Many families are often sharply divided, due to their workers' migrations and social class achievements, so that the more self-contained nuclear units eventually cut themselves off from meaningful contacts with their extended kin groups. These changes decrease the importance of elders in family cultures, and overload the emotional intensity of relationships within the varied family fragments. For example, many nuclear families became so emotionally overloaded that they disintegrate or break down.

A more positive view of the influences of modernization and secularization on families is that economic industrialization frees families to enter more whole-heartedly into market dynamics, and to increase their possibilities of economic success. At the same time, family members became freer to honor their own religious beliefs in their family cultures, being less beholden to the religious domination of members of older generations. Family members also increasingly see themselves as citizens of societies, rather than members of their declining local communities.

It is against a backdrop of these kinds of historical changes that we need to understand our family, community, and societal cultures, and the continuing impacts they have on how we live. The cultures of modernization and secularization bring widespread insecurities, as well as freedoms, and we now have even more ethical obligations to make responsible choices for ourselves, our families, and coming generations. Only when we see our cultures more clearly can we think through why our families are important, how to build or maintain strong families, and how to work toward increasing social justice for all.

V. Families and Society

When modernization and secularization changed families' and societies' cultures, the scope of societies broadened, and an increased awareness of globalization developed. As a result, recent trend data suggest that nation states do not necessarily have the impermeable boundaries they used to have. For example, racial and ethnic groups frequently cut across countries, as do economic classes, gender classes, and cultural patterns.

Contemporary societies press us to think more inclusively about the realities and possibilities of an international community, with some appreciation that whatever goes on within countries is at least in part a consequence of those particular countries' standings in international relations. This is especially apparent in comparisons of economic means, scientific discoveries, and accumulations of power. Similarly we have an increased awareness that families are affected not only by how they cope and thrive in a particular society, but also by how strong the families are in their countries, and in the world.

We increase our social intelligence when we consider the impact of these broad societal perspectives on understanding connections between individuals, their own families, families in a specific society, and families in the world. Social intelligence helps us to understand more fully how we are affected by complex, overlapping social influences, as well as how whatever we do has repercussions for these interlocking social spheres. Although it is difficult to measure the extent and effects of this interdependence accurately, we can identify some trends and patterns of behavior in how families cope and thrive. Furthermore, we find that merely considering these broad national, international, and global social influences enables us to increase our control over our lives.

The contemporary forces that move us toward globalization are multi-faceted. However, the dominance of both global economics and global politics has a longstanding historical reality, and there appears to be no stopping human urges to travel, explore, and conquer. Even though some variations in these patterns may appear to be qualitatively distinct, the global economy has developed and thrives largely because of intense national and international competition.

One of the main characteristics of individual families is that they are emotional systems. Families are emotional systems not only because most are essentially small groups, but also because emotions are omnipresent in social exchanges, and especially in intimate, personal exchanges. Thus we are emotional beings in our most intimate relations, as well as in our wars, and in our fiercest competitions with others. Our families are vulnerable to emotions which are both within and external to them. However, we continue to move toward globalization because we have economic, political, and emotional needs to adapt to other societies through cooperative efforts to maintain world security and world peace.

One of the ways in which families cope, in light of the strength of these influences, is that they use a "we" and "they" dynamic. For example, families often close ranks emotionally, in order to deal more effectively with outsiders and outside influences. Although this may not be productive for families in the long run, in that their resulting relationships become too intense and emotionally overloaded, our "we" and "they" assignations often simplify and clarify our complex allegiances, so that they become more manageable.

Our awareness about what goes on in society, and in the world, is also strongly influenced by modern mass media. Mass media have added momentum to the global information revolution, and one impact of media communications on families is that facts about societies are frequently magnified or distorted. This makes it difficult for families to know the truth about which complex social influences make important differences in their lives, even though they may realize that these impacts exist. When the overwhelming reality of global society overshadows families and their individual members, their increased senses of powerlessness in relation to the world make family problems more likely. Therefore, we need to strengthen our families, so they will be more immune to societal pressures, and sufficiently balanced to enter into enterprises that increase the common good.

Even though it is difficult to assess historical trends in societies and the world, our freedom is often based on being able to do so. We cannot resist debilitating family emotions or others' exploitation effectively, until we know where we stand in the total scheme of things, as well as what our options are. Furthermore we cannot be responsible for our own families, and others' well-being, unless we have the freedom to act autonomously. The interdependence of family well-being and the common good makes it possible for social intelligence to help us to deal with these dilemmas. Social intelligence helps us to become historical actors as family members, as members of societies, and as members of the world community.

Globalization

Conventional thinking does not easily connect our families to globalization, or globalization to our families. In fact, most people do not see many important connections between our families and societies, or societal trends and our families. However, social intelligence builds vital knowledge and know-how about these connections, and also requires us to take seriously the global social contexts of our personal lives.

One of the results of globalization this last century is a relative decrease in some national and local interests, together with a relative increase in the long-term trend of community breakdown. When societies concentrate on building international relations, as well as on establishing diversity in national education and occupations, some of the special interests of families and communities are overlooked. Because the broadest interests of societies, such as maintaining active participation in contemporary globalization, are directly connected to their common good, priorities must be developed which maintain the common good and at the same time meet both local and global needs.

Just as it is important for families to teach their children about their own religions, ethnicities, races, neighborhoods, towns, and countries, so that they become well-integrated with their societies, it is also important to help families to see the world as it is. Members of our youngest generations need to understand the historical realities of their era, in order to avoid the destructive distortions that develop from lofty ideals and euphemisms about international relations.

One way for families to connect globalization to local concerns is to use their daily experiences of religious, international, racial, ethnic, and economic diversity as opportunities to teach their children about the richness and strengths of human varieties in the world. This kind of learning goes beyond attending different kinds of cultural events, because it focuses on getting to know or working with people who are from diverse backgrounds. The increased openness and flexibility of families who do this strengthens them, and improves our societies of tomorrow.

Families' awareness of their societies is perpetually filtered by their societies' international relations. Conditions in the world at large affect both global and national trends in birth rates, divorces, migrations, illnesses, and health. Thus we are who we are in part because we are advantaged or disadvantaged by global trends, as well as by international patterns of gender, race, and ethnic relations. Given these intrinsic insecurities, social intelligence provides us with a useful and reliable orientation, because it is built on our awareness of our interdependence at all levels of social organization in and among societies.

V. Families and Society

One of the contemporary challenges for families in globalization is for them to lead societies by focusing on both local and global interests. Just as it is important for families to adapt to complex trends within their societies, it is also beneficial for families to respond to familial, local, and national needs in globalization. Thus well-functioning families develop capacities to stay meaningfully connected not only to their own kin groups, but also to their kin members' homelands. Families who accomplish this degree of openness and connection become sufficiently strong to lead other families in orienting their children to give meaningful service to others, for example, as well as in building or rebuilding local communities.

All too often the emotional systems of families are so intense that they prevent their family members from seeing the larger realities of societies and globalization. This restricts families' abilities to guide their members toward taking action in the world. On the other hand, globalization cannot be the sole goal of family members, if real family needs are to be met. It is important that we balance our energies, so that local, national, and international needs can be addressed at least to some extent at different stages of our lives. Social intelligence helps us to understand the competing stresses of demands on our attention, and guides us to be practical in our responses to family, national, and global social realities.

When we are able to see, and more fully understand, this broader picture of our lives, we realize the shared necessity to tackle social justice issues in our societies and the world. As aware individuals and families, we have responsibilities to improve social conditions for ourselves and for others, as well as to make constructive contributions to a common good that reaches beyond national self-interest. Although there are many disagreements on how to go about accomplishing these goals, social intelligence gives us a sufficiently firm foothold to start our challenging journeys in this direction.

Global Economics

One important aspect of globalization, which has a major impact on all societies, is the global economy. In the last century the world shifted from being made up of many different economies—sometimes in single societies, sometimes in groups of countries—to being a more or less unified world economy. The market forces which govern this interdependent global economy derive primarily from capitalism.

Our global economy reinforces stratification systems based on financial means. Families' economies depend on national and international market forces, even though some of the international aspects of domestic economies are often hidden from families, or not understood by families, as they make their daily purchases. Unless we are unusually well-informed, we do not necessarily realize the patterns of international production that enter into the broad array of goods and services that we and our families consume.

Global economics have transformed our family dynamics. Historically families produced many or most of their own needed goods and services, but in modern societies families became their own kinds of units of consumption. Families purchase what they need or want for their survival and fulfillment, and they usually look to commercial sources to meet as many of their goods and service needs as they can afford. Consequently, our patterns of purchasing particular items depend more on our financial means than on our labor skills. This contrasts with the past, when our work directly supported our existence, as well as our opportunities to get ahead in life.

The global economy, which is increasingly organized as a vast exchange system based on complex divisions of labor, may exert stronger influences on our family behavior than national economies. Related to the significance of global economic realities is the fact that in many respects our independence from our families is measured by, or reflects, our economic independence. For example, we often do not consider adults to be fully mature until they can support themselves financially.

V. Families and Society

Furthermore, marriage, which historically was considered to be a sign of adulthood, is frequently discouraged unless one or both partners have sufficient economic means to support themselves and their future children.

Because of the dominance of economic factors in significant aspects of family life, family members tend to remain emotionally dependent on others when they are not economically self-sufficient. This prolonged emotional dependence limits opportunities in life, and perpetuates childlike relationships and goals, unless at the same time a gradual transition is made toward economic independence. Families benefit from raising children who become economically independent in their own right, as this is essentially a necessary condition of other family members' own freedom and autonomy for crucial life choices.

Another way in which the global economy has a lasting impact on possibilities for families is the kinds of skills that family members are encouraged to develop in order to become financially independent. It is strategic to send children to prestigious schools and colleges, but parents also need to be concerned about the future earnings of their children. Unfortunately capitalist market forces often present somewhat limited choices to young adults who want to map out creative new ventures, because economic stability results largely from establishment-oriented, routine jobs.

Geographical mobility, often linked to job choices, threatens the unity of nuclear families and their kin groups, and in a global economy professional positions are increasingly accompanied by travel abroad, or even migrations. Unless our families place a high priority on maintaining meaningful contacts with their relatives, many families will be increasingly fragmented by these economic pressures and demands.

Even where market labor is not clearly related to the global economy, the demands of the global economy can infiltrate the quality of families' work days and leisure activities. When local companies are in competition with other companies in national and international markets, for example, the pressure to work long hours is strong and unrelenting. These kinds of work day demands present problems for all families, because families do not thrive well when their most competent adult members are absent. Even though individual families' special arrangements may appear to be viable, the long range effects of these economic pressures on most marriages and children can be detrimental to the well-being of whole families.

Social intelligence helps us to see these patterns and tendencies in the global economy and in our families, and at the same time guides us to take steps to neutralize their negative consequences. For example, social intelligence suggests possibilities for creating stronger families that resist, or cope effectively with, the pressures of living and working in a global economy. When we know how to deal with the emotional systems of our work places, as well as our families, we are less likely to turn to divorce or other dramatic but sometimes harmful means to resolve what we had previously thought were interpersonal tensions. Our families are important to us, as well as to our societies, and we need to treat them with as much enlightenment and care as possible.

Global Politics

In many respects societies' political power reflects the amount of economic resources societies have. Economic assets and political power overlap considerably, so that the two spheres of global economics and global politics frequently have similar patterns in international relations. However, some aspects of global politics and global power have distinctive ramifications for families.

The broadest aspects of global politics raise questions about power in societal coalitions, particularly with regard to who makes decisions about the use of legitimate force—sometimes warfare—in societies or groups of societies. In democracies, these issues are traditionally determined by popular votes. Thus, when social conflicts are resolved by force within and between societies, those with decision-making powers about the uses of force are not necessarily the wealthiest members of society.

V. Families and Society

Combinations of economic and political powers in the global sphere easily overwhelm the necessarily limited autonomy of families. Furthermore, even though global politics may be nominally democratic, families' votes do not determine actual outcomes. Consequently, the relative powerlessness of families—in contrast to global economic and political powers—is felt acutely. This does not mean, however, that families should withdraw from national and global political realities, but rather that family members should build awareness, within and among families, of alternative ways to influence or cope with political outcomes.

Women's and minority groups' experiences suggest that politics, even global politics, are not only produced by governments, but also express complex grassroots interpersonal and family exchanges. Thus politics are both public and intensely personal, especially because power relations influence how we run our families, and how we define interdependence and independence within our families. Social intelligence helps us to discover these subtle, sometimes hidden, dimensions of power that influence whatever we do in our families and in societies. Locating both power and powerlessness within our families, for example, is a useful starting point for unraveling the mysteries and hidden aspects of the more public power dimensions that permeate our societies and families.

As in the global sphere, family politics may evolve from the use of force by the dominant few in our families. Such coercion increases the probability of family abuse and family violence. When intimidation and family violence exist, social intelligence helps us to find effective ways to intervene, as well as to prevent or interrupt sequences of destructive behavior, so that we can eventually free ourselves from such threats. It is because families are so important in their own right that the politics of force—in local, national, and international relations—are particularly troubling, and need our close attention and intervention in order to achieve social justice.

One reason why abuse and violence are repeated, in different generations of our families, is that the visibility of violence and abuse, at national and international levels, reinforces abusive and violent behavior within our families. These disastrous broad social realities legitimate unacceptable behavior among intimates, so that effective interventions and conflict resolutions often become increasingly difficult to accomplish. Furthermore, we tend to accept too many problematic sexual and interpersonal codes of behavior among men and women, which frequently lead to abuse and violence. This happens because it is often hard to determine when and how lines should be drawn regarding the exercise of power or force in personal relationships as well as political relations.

In wartime, global politics are expressed in extreme ways, and many seriously destructive aspects of power become apparent. In addition to accumulations of powerful arms and munitions, which intimidate or ultimately terrorize masses of individuals and families, ethnic cleansing and genocide may occur. We fear for our lives in wartime, because we all suffer from the effects and consequences of large-scale, random injustices and violence.

Families have to cope with crisis conditions when their young adults go into military service during wars. These families are inevitably heavily burdened by their tremendous sacrifices, if only through the absences of their active, adult members. When war casualties occur, or family losses become permanent, these families may not be able to recover sufficiently to protect their young and old relatives again.

Social intelligence enables us to be more aware of some of these complex aspects of global politics, and their influences on our families. We need to pause and reflect on the likely consequences of our decisions before we make them, so that we can be more realistically prepared for whatever evolves. Ideally global politics do not determine who we are, or what we do. For example, we can use emotional or spiritual resources to help us to transcend the horrors of war and destruction when needed. However, in both war and peace, global politics inevitably influence how we conduct ourselves within our families, and how we transmit our world views and values to members of our youngest generations.

Mass Media

Mass media have made communications within and between societies quick and easy. Although both the hard copy and electronic content of mass media communications contain many biases and distortions, which make it difficult for consumers to know what is factual or accurate, the numbers of meaningful connections among societies have increased because of these widespread, pervasive exchanges. National headlines and international news, for example, help us to realize our dependence on others, especially due to our shared similar or related historical circumstances.

Because mass media can be used expressly to manipulate and exploit members of societies, discretion and critical thinking about media content are constantly necessary for our own protection, and for saving lives. Political propaganda frequently serves only the interests of those in power, for example, so this must be treated with extreme caution. Family initiatives and leadership are needed to protect children and vulnerable family members from such unwanted exploitation and oppression.

Large commercial conglomerates, with their capacities to advertise widely, must also be treated critically. For example, advertisements often cultivate artificial senses of unity among their audiences, at the same time strongly suggesting that we need to purchase particular products in order to enjoy life, or to meet needs which we do not really have. We should also be aware that some of these unifying powers of mass media in societies are dangerous, because they make populations increasingly vulnerable to political exploitations on a massive scale.

The fact that mass media can communicate a wide diversity of cultures to their audiences means that they have the potential to be both enlightening and educational. We undoubtedly benefit from knowing more about how others think and manage their societies. In these respects mass media may accomplish a great deal, as well as increase our awareness of families in relation to current affairs in our societies and the world. Acquiring this increased knowledge about contemporary events and social conditions is a very significant part of building social intelligence.

Families receive a wide variety of mass media presentations in their homes. Information from daily newscasts and current affairs educates children about the world, and helps to develop their social intelligence about themselves and others. We cannot teach our children only about our own families, because this insular perspective narrows children's lives rather than broadens them. Although we started to learn about the world first by hearing family histories from our relatives, as adults we are responsible for opening up the worlds of our children and others.

One way to accomplish these goals is to help our children to develop critical postures to the content of mass media. For example, we deliberately show them how we use particular media sources which we know are relatively trustworthy and reliable. Thus, our real leadership of younger generation members comes from teaching them how to be critical about mass media, rather than by policing their consumption of mass media.

A dangerous aspect of the unifying powers of mass media is the particularly strong impact that media have on our children and adolescents. For example, television programs and their advertisements target young children by showing stories or characters in violent settings, or by portraying glitzy toys which are not in children's long term interests. These programs and advertisements often make children believe that real life is reflected in these carefully selected media images, or persuade them that they need particular products. By so doing, corporations and advertising agencies influence their youngest consumers through using attractive, but basically harmful or meaningless images, to capture their attention. Although both our children and adolescents benefit from some media productions, they are also negatively influenced by mass media's many powerful effects, especially through their impacts on their long term, lifetime spending habits.

Whole families are also targeted by mass media interests, so that they too remain vulnerable to their exploitation. However, our families may also grow stronger, in some respects, because of the compelling powers of mass media: we learn about contemporary events like never before; it is easier to understand world diversity through media presentations; and we become more aware of, and more critical of, media exploitations. Our families also benefit from continuing developments in direct personal electronic communications. For example, kin unity is enhanced by easy and inexpensive telephone or email exchanges among our relatives.

It is highly unlikely that societal trends in the grasp of mass media on our attention will decline or be reversed. It appears that we live in historic times when the media will increasingly permeate the quality of our daily lives. This means that we have to be correspondingly vigilant—by using social intelligence—about the impacts of media images and media biases on our families. Social intelligence also suggests how to make wiser value choices for ourselves and our families in mass media's ever-present social influences.

Family Trends

Family trends are patterned or measured family behavior within and among societies. Family trends are frequently calculated as bases for political purposes and decision-making: for example, to make comparisons of behavior in different times and different places, in order to assess social changes, so that political policies will meet particular needs. Family trends include demographic assessments of births, deaths, or migrations, as well as assessments of family behavior in relation to social class, education, economic achievement, religion, ethnicity, race, gender, or age.

Family trends often pinpoint some of the different rhythms of societies that influence the individual workings of families.

Families' emotional systems are not created in vacuums, but rather emerge in part as responses to external and internal social pressures. However, family trends in societies do not determine, but rather influence, how we relate to other family members, and how we make significant life course decisions, such as when we marry or the number of children we have.

Some of the broadest family trends that influenced internal patterns of family behavior were those caused by the industrial revolution. These family trends included migrations of family members or entire families to cities, in order to take advantage of new jobs in the machine age; separations between nuclear families and their extended kin groups during and after these migrations; and increased marked differences in the work responsibilities of men and women, women being paid considerably less for their industrial labors than men. Because we usually consider only contemporary family trends in societies, we often take these historical trends for granted, without questioning their social origins and social impacts.

As standards of living were raised by the widespread consumption of products and discoveries of the industrial revolution, the growing middle class gained momentum and placed a higher value on education, emphasizing the education of women as well as men. More women gained economic and emotional independence, and after two world wars divorce rates soared, partly because these lethal upheavals and political strife predisposed both women and men to want companionship in their marriages, which they were increasingly willing and able to change partners to get.

Accompanying trends related to some of these changes include increased secularization, where religious and traditional standards were questioned, and in some cases abandoned. Discoveries in contraception, as well as the legalization of abortion, further increased the independence of women and men, and ties to the older generations of family members were irretrievably weakened. In these respects, families in the Western hemisphere initially grew more unlike families in the

East, where filial piety or loyalty to elders remained as a relatively important cultural value.

Social intelligence requires a minimum working knowledge of these kinds of historical family trends, within and among societies, which have affected our families deeply. Social intelligence is also built on understanding how family patterns throughout societies affect families. We do not live in social vacuums, and our families are not independently produced solely by their own family members. For better or for worse, we and our families are affected by societal trends. Even if we actively resist trends we do not want, or do not agree with, we are still influenced by them. Our successes in opposing societal trends often depend on our social intelligence about the nature of the trends we oppose, as well as on our emotional courage and astuteness, especially with regard to taking effective collective action. Furthermore, we need to understand the social dynamics of our opposition as fully as possible, in order to create viable alternatives.

Our families are influenced by such a wide range of social influences, that fighting off particular trends does not necessarily free us from them. We need to be aware of both constructive and destructive social trends, and at the same time develop families that will support and inspire their members to become citizens of neighborhoods, societies, and the world. How we do this is one of the main questions that *Families and Social Intelligence* seeks to answer, especially because social intelligence can play a crucial role in accomplishing such a daunting and challenging task.

In order to increase our social intelligence, we must reflect upon the importance of families to us personally, and to the survival of communities and societies. We should also consider our daily behavior as responses to social influences—families, beliefs, social classes, cultures, and societies—and most particularly to the emotional pressures of these influences. When we understand some of the complexity of our social realities, we can begin to unravel our entrapment in social trends, in order to rebuild significant parts of ourselves and our families.

Learning social intelligence helps us to solve our families' problems by showing us how to think through some of our families' most critical dilemmas. When we use social intelligence to guide our actions, we become less emotionally reactive to others and societal trends. Consequently, we make more enlightened assessments of ourselves, our families, and our societies, thereby increasing our freedom and independence in our families and in our societies.

Family Problems

Most of us do not examine our families or societies closely unless we are trying to deal with some challenging or persisting problems. Furthermore, even though we may wrestle with the same or similar family problems year by year, we are often reluctant to look at the whole of our families, or the whole of our societies, as influencing our situations. It is easier for us to think in individual terms—to blame someone else for our problems; to think of personality as a fixed constellation of innate qualities that cannot be changed; or to resolve family issues by leaving our families in order to begin new relationships—rather than to scrutinize the impacts of social influences in our lives.

Social intelligence offers different approaches to understanding and dealing with family issues. For example, when we understand the complexities of our families' and societies' effects on our particular situations, we are more able to make constructive decisions for ourselves and others. We use social intelligence to understand our families, in order to gain more control over our everyday routines, and to become more adept at changing our own behavior and circumstances when necessary.

Social intelligence gives us broader views of who we and our families are in society than is usually considered when dealing with problematic personal relationships or family issues. Developing our social intelligence helps us to see the reactivity of the emotional systems to which we belong, as well as the extent to which our beliefs define our daily situations and world views. When we are socially intelligent we more capably assess the impact of social classes on who we and our relatives think we are, for example, as well as see connections between social classes, cultures, and societies. As we broaden our perspectives on our lives, we increase our objectivity, and we understand what it takes to be historical actors in the world.

Some of our motivations to change our perceptions of ourselves and our societies flow from our determination to help our families to become more open and more flexible in their relationships. When our strategies are guided by social intelligence, it is more likely that our family members will be more comfortable, and have more freedoms. When we succeed in opening up our family relationships in this way, for example, we go a long way toward resolving varied family problems, especially those that previously limited flexibility and freedom in our families.

Using social intelligence to deepen our appreciation of the importance of families, to individuals and to societies, is another significant step toward resolving family problems. This does not mean that our families are more worthy than others' families, but rather that being a family member is a widely-shared experience, that tends to level social class differences among people. When we understand that our families are emotional systems that react to internal and external pressures, for example, we see some of the similarities that exist among all families more clearly.

Being an active participant in the social institution of families is a deep-seated challenge, whether we prefer traditional or modern families. However, the end point of deepening our appreciation of the complexity of our families is not merely to resolve our own family problems. The longer term, more transcendental and more idealistic objectives, are first to establish sufficient freedom throughout our own families, which gradually resolves many different kinds of family problems, and then to address other issues which are related more directly to other families and the common good.

Working on problems in our own families is an effective preparation for increasing freedom in society. We increase our social intelligence, as well as strengthen our capacities to act autonomously, when we take our families seriously, and work toward ameliorating their conditions, relationships, and actions. Understanding the importance of families is significant because families are crucibles of human behavior. Becoming more responsible in our families enables us to work toward social justice, as well as to assume more effective leadership positions in societies.

In examining family problems, we need to know which family members suffer the most from these problems, and who contributes the most to the problems. In addition, we must realize that additional family imbalances may result from the specific adjustments we made to resolve problematic issues. For example, if family members use social intelligence to challenge their dominant family members, resistance to such a challenge is predictable. Family members who have vested interests in the status quo will unite to restore the families' emotional systems to their former equilibriums, and will label their upstart family members as problems. Ideally, family members who act to limit their relatives' dominance understand that a certain amount of disruption and resistance are unavoidable consequences of their changes, which will eventually move these whole families toward increased social justice.

Socially intelligent, holistic approaches to solving family problems become clearer when we look at how social intelligence guides us and our families. The next four chapters of *Families and Social Intelligence* outline specific strategies to increase the social intelligence of individuals and families, and to accomplish freeing changes in our families.

Social Intelligence and Families

VI. What Difference Does Social Intelligence Make?

S ocial intelligence is the capacity to think and act from social systems perspectives. This learned, partially experiential knowledge is built by developing an awareness of the most significant social influences in our everyday lives, and their impacts on our behavior. The particular social sources of our emotions—some of the most deep-seated aspects of our individual and social being—which are examined in *Families and Social Intelligence* are our families, beliefs, social classes, cultures, and societies. These are basic dimensions of social intelligence, which we can choose to strengthen and increase— or neglect and decrease—throughout our lives.

One of the differences that social intelligence makes is that we can use its principles to guide our decision-making and everyday behavior. When we know why we behave in certain ways, we are freer to make our necessary daily choices, and more free to choose what we really want to accomplish in the long run. We can use our social intelligence to add meaning to our exchanges with others, for example, or to pursue goals which both meet our needs and contribute to the common good.

A beneficial result of being guided by social intelligence is that we essentially wake up to our own social realities, and see the world for what it is. Social intelligence increases our objectivity, as well as broadens our views of ourselves, others, societies, and the world. Once we see the complexity of social relations that permeates our individuality, as well as the conditions of our shared existence, we are less likely to succumb to others' views of what they consider to be important. Thus, becoming more socially aware makes us less vulnerable to the manipulation or oppression of others' self interests.

Social intelligence has a strong, enlightening influence on how we see our families, and on how we interact with them. The fact-based approach of social intelligence—which we test by our own experiences as much as possible—enables us to discard many of the dogmatic, overly sentimental views of families which dominate our cultures. Our beliefs about our families should be challenged and supported by as many facts as possible, if we are to make mature decisions based on social intelligence.

Everyone has some degree of social intelligence because each of us needs social intelligence to become human, to be socialized successfully, and to survive. Our particular levels of learned social intelligence vary according to our families, beliefs, social classes, cultures, and societies. However, unless we deliberately use our social intelligence on a daily basis—increase it through learning about social influences, and apply it to varied social situations—we risk letting our social intelligence atrophy and diminish. Continuing to work at expanding our social intelligence allows us to live more fully.

When we use social intelligence habitually, or even before these practices are fully developed, our resulting breadth of vision enables us to see ourselves more clearly as historical actors. Knowing that we are products of our families, beliefs, social classes, cultures, and societies empowers us by making us more aware of possibilities to change our individual and social destinies. When we realize that we learn social intelligence through our experiences and studies, we are no longer trapped in fatalistic views of history or globalization. Optimally, becoming historical actors means that we act—as individuals and as groups—in ways that improve ourselves and the world.

The fact that social intelligence enables us to become constructive historical actors raises the issue of how this moral imperative can be applied to our everyday lives. One way to become historical actors is to learn from others who have taken courageous, responsible social actions that increased social justice.

This focus helps us to realize the wide range of choices that constantly await us on our many different paths. For example, we may choose not only to meet our own families' needs, but also to formulate family policies or other social strategies to increase the common good of all families. When we make commitments to increase our social intelligence, as well as to allow our actions to be inspired by social intelligence, one of the greatest differences this orientation makes is that we can proceed more effectively toward achieving social justice.

Families as Foundations

In reflecting about the five selected dimensions or strands of social intelligence—families, beliefs, social classes, cultures, and societies—it is worthwhile to remember that even though all of these dimensions interrelate, and represent a powerful sum of significant social influences in our lives, none is more important than our families. This is so because the ways in which we become human—for better or for worse—are through the initial impact of our family relationships, as well as through their continuing patterns of interaction. The longest lasting social influences on our behavior frequently emerge from continuities in our families' interactions, especially as most of us deal with family exchanges of one kind or another until we die.

Our initial and enduring family exchanges with our relatives range from being positive to being negative, or from being constructive to being destructive. Regardless of the specific kinds of family interactions within these contrasts, they are consistently powerful influences on our social being, goals, and ideals. We frequently continue to strive for the same values as our families, for example, as we make our way through the varied demands of our adult lives. A related characteristic of our family legacies is that they are deeply emotional, representing the whole gamut of different degrees and different kinds of emotions. Our deepest learned emotions and feelings are largely products of the emotional systems of our earliest, past, and relatively recent patterns of family interaction.

Social intelligence accounts for the emotional dominance of our families by considering our families to be the most basic foundations of our social intelligence. This means that our beliefs, social classes, cultures, and societies have the impacts they do largely as consequences of the emotional conditioning and pressures we received, and still receive, from our family systems. We are who we are first and foremost because of what went on, and what still happens, in our families' emotional systems. Our most basic levels of social intelligence derive from our responses to our families' unique patterns of behavior.

Once the foundation of our social intelligence is created by our knowledge and awareness of the ways in which we participate in our families, the four additional strands of social intelligence influence this foundation. However, although beliefs, social classes, cultures, and societies necessarily modify the family foundations of our social intelligence to some extent, the main players in our families—which include ourselves— continue to have the most powerful influences on what we do, largely because of the intensity of the emotions that are activated by our family exchanges and relationships.

Our families are not only our first powerful social experiences, but they also continue to exert considerable emotional significance and power on our behavior whatever beliefs, social classes, cultures, and societies we encounter in our current and future situations. Our families remain as our home bases for our awareness of self and our socially intelligent know-how, to which we are compelled to return because of the intensity of our families' positive or negative emotional systems, regardless of our material circumstances. This does not mean that other individual and group experiences cannot significantly change our family influences. External social influences, largely unrelated to our families, challenge us continuously.

VI. What Difference Does Social Intelligence Make?

Another aspect of the interdependence of our family influences, as well as other social influences, is that if we decide to change what we do, including how we operate in our families, our family changes directly affect the influences of our beliefs, social classes, cultures, and societies. This means that one of our most important tasks, in increasing our social intelligence, is to continue to try to change the emotional dynamics of our families. When we and other relatives are substantially free and autonomous in our families, we meet our real individual and social needs more effectively, as well as achieve increased social justice in society.

In order to gain this position of strength, we must persevere in working on our family relationships as high priorities. We need to remember, for example, that because of our emotional entanglements with our families, they are more difficult to deal with than other social groups. Even though our families share some similarities with other groups, our families' lifetime memberships, their blood links or contractual bonds, as well as their long individual and social histories, make them unique and especially demanding. These qualities give our families more emotional and cultural power over us than any other groups. Our families also continue to be influential because only they try to meet our dependency needs at all stages of our life cycles.

Practicing social intelligence in our everyday lives requires us to at least temporarily suspend our conventional judgments that our families do not exert significant power over us. This allows us to entertain the idea that our families have considerable power over us more seriously, so that we can begin to see the pervasiveness of family influences in our lives and in our societies more clearly. Our suspensions of conventional judgments also enable us to become more aware that we harbor a wide range of different cultural expectations about how families are supposed to be, even though these specifics may not ring true with respect to our own particular family experiences.

The fact that cultural or societal family beliefs and expectations exist means that we are frequently pressured to compare and contrast our family experiences with those of other people. Furthermore, we often become preoccupied with these family comparisons. This is additional evidence of families' emotional significance, and of the emotional hold our families have over how we think and what we do.

Beliefs and Motivations

A second dimension of social intelligence, our beliefs, bridges family processes and our participation in communities. Our beliefs include particular belief systems, such as religions, politics, ideologies, and science, as well as more fragmented beliefs. Sacred and secular sets of beliefs are routinely modified by individuals and families, and have a wide range of impacts on our behavior. For example, belief systems vary in their effects from being no more than lip service to a particular tradition, to being an entire way of life for a lifetime, or several generations. Whatever the intensity of our beliefs, they share some basic characteristics: they have social origins; they provide us with world views; they are based on assumptions about human nature; they have the power, or at least the potential, to guide and influence our behavior; and they motivate how we conduct ourselves on a daily basis.

Just as social intelligence gives us increased objectivity about the social origins and emotional components of our patterns of family interaction, social intelligence also gives us increased objectivity about the social origins and emotional components of our most significant beliefs and motivations. Because social intelligence helps us to think more clearly about the power and complexity of social influences, we need to analyze and deliberately choose our most cherished beliefs and motivations, if we are to increase our freedom. Unless we do this, others' social and emotional influences will dominate and perhaps exploit our actions. Social intelligence helps us to get more in charge of what we do, and may even help us to turn our lives around.

Traditions assign sacredness to the religions we are taught in our families. However, social intelligence requires that we ask

VI. What Difference Does Social Intelligence Make?

significant questions about our religious beliefs, such as who decided that we would be raised in particular religions, and why the children in our families have been raised in the same or different religions over generations. Some of these answers, especially from the point of view of social intelligence, provide us with social rather than theological reasons for our religious beliefs. For example, we become religious through our religious socialization, rather than through divine intervention. Although the fact that we were raised in specific religions may be largely due to arbitrary circumstances, the content of our beliefs depends mostly on who taught us what during our early religious socialization.

Even though, as adults, we know that we have many more choices about how we worship, as well as what aspects of our religions we believe, relatively few adults convert to alternative religions, unless there are significant religious or secular concerns like raising children in interfaith marriages. For the most part, families' religious socialization is so influential that adult children often seek only partners with the same religious beliefs, later dying in that same religious tradition.

This example of religions as beliefs, with their tendencies of persistence and continuities, shows us not only that our beliefs are very significant social dimensions of who we are, but also that religious or social motivations can govern how we act for a lifetime. Religions are often important aspects of our individual and social being because families control what and how their children learn both religious and secular beliefs. Social intelligence helps us to disentangle some of the overlapping family and social influences we experience in learning our religious beliefs, and enables us to see what our options are with respect to these complex social realities.

When religious beliefs are fueled by emotional intensity, or by fundamentalist religiosity, they become a clear but extreme example of the tremendous power that beliefs may have over our actions. Secular beliefs, because they do not draw directly from sacred beliefs, or use sacred sanctions to motivate actions, are usually less influential. However, in some instances, secular beliefs—such as ideologies or science—may prove to be equally as strong as religious beliefs in their impacts on our actions.

Social intelligence is a useful tool to help us to compare and contrast the many different kinds of beliefs that we hold, to define our beliefs' social origins, and to see how particular individuals influenced us to take major directions in our lives— such as specific jobs or careers. As we become more objective about our beliefs and motivations, social intelligence helps us to identify ways in which we can loosen the tight hold of religious and secular beliefs that do not meet our current or future needs.

Social intelligence, with its central concern for increasing social justice through strengthening the common good, highlights the importance of deliberately selecting beliefs that motivate us to act in these directions. Our critical objectivity about social influences helps us to design ways to assess whether our religious or secular beliefs provide us with truths we can live by, or whether we should choose alternative beliefs and motivations to guide us.

Social Class Confines

A third dimension of social intelligence is social classes' influences on our being and doing. Particularly important are the limits that social class memberships impose on us, formally or informally. Even though we may not consider that our social classes seriously restrict what we can or cannot do, these particular social influences can narrow our perceptions and behavior in significant ways. Because lacks of serious consideration about social classes occur frequently, we need to include our own social class awareness as a critical aspect of deliberately increasing our social intelligence.

We start to strengthen our social intelligence about social classes by being more objective in considering the wide range of possibilities for social class memberships—social classes may be based on economic means, educational achievement, gender, sexual orientation, race, ethnicity, or able-bodiedness— and the ways in which these classifications affect us. Our

VI. What Difference Does Social Intelligence Make?

increased objectivity enables us to see how prejudice and discrimination restrict social mobility between social classes, for example. Objectivity also enables us to assess the extent to which our views of social class confines are imagined rather than real. This is useful because imagined social class confines are often much easier to change than if they are factual. Although it is challenging and difficult to increase our understanding of all the subtleties of social class restrictions, social intelligence shows us that many individuals and groups have successfully overcome both imagined and real barriers of prejudice and discrimination.

It is worthwhile to strive to build our social intelligence about social classes because these social influences are widespread and problematic. Becoming more socially intelligent about our social classes enables us to do something about how social classes influence us. For example, recognizing and neutralizing the impacts of social class differences makes us freer. Even when we choose only that our new freedoms from social classes will not merely enable us to be upwardly mobile, we become less impeded by social class limitations.

Thus social intelligence makes a difference by neutralizing many of the pernicious consequences of our social classes. Whatever social class bases we consider, in order to assess which social classes affect us the most, we gain some freedom and autonomy when we examine each of our social classes from perspectives of social intelligence. Being socially intelligent about our social class memberships, as well as being socially intelligent about what these social classes mean in our lives, helps us to be more objective about the social conditions that characterize our social class memberships.

Although the substance and patterns of individuals' and families' social class differences based on economic means, educational achievement, gender, sexual orientation, race, ethnicity, or able-bodiedness vary widely, there are some common denominators among the "have" or "have-not" dimensions of these social classes. For example, it is usually restrictions to social class mobility—such as prejudice and discrimination—that hold the hierarchies of stratification systems in place. We not only have to meet certain criteria for class membership, but we also have to gain the approval of those who are already members of the social classes to which we aspire, if we are to be socially mobile.

Social intelligence helps us to articulate the negative consequences of social classes, and suggests that moving in directions of social justice neutralizes some of these negative social class influences. When we orient our behavior and goals toward ideals of social justice, we at the same time cease to perpetuate some of the inherent injustices of social classes. Because social intelligence is a body of knowledge about basic social influences that we can use to guide our behavior, we redefine our situations when we aim to construct improved futures that reduce social class limitations, especially if at the same time we try to increase the common good and social justice.

History has been described as a series of social class conflicts, which endorses the power and social significance that social classes have on the quality of our lives through time. There is no doubt that social classes are forces in their own right, which exist both because of, and in spite of, our individual and collective decisions. Seeing our own social class situations in these broad perspectives enables us to be more effective historical actors, who both recognize and deal with the power of these compelling, moving forces.

Culture and Power

Culture, a fourth strand of social intelligence, is an additional combination of complex social influences that affects us deeply. Culture is so deeply ingrained in our being and doing that it permeates what we take for granted, as well as presents us with the only means we have available to think through who we are and what our lives mean. Therefore, we cannot easily discern the essential issues of our human identity without at the same time considering what our cultures are, and the impacts they have on all stages of our being.

Culture is both visible and invisible. By giving serious attention to culture, social intelligence helps us to sort out the more obvious cultural influences that have shaped us, from those that are more difficult to see. Social intelligence also enables us to understand the important, relatively invisible cultural influence of the combined effects of culture and power. Furthermore, social intelligence requires us to understand how our cultural priorities, such as our ideals, have been formed, and how our families and their patterns of social or emotional dominance have affected us. It is only when we see these complex but powerful social influences more clearly, that we discover whose values and goals we have absorbed and called our own.

Becoming socially intelligent makes many significant differences to us because we learn how culture permeates our perceptions of what is normal and what is ideal, as well as how our perceptions and actions have been influenced by the leadership of those who taught us our cultures. When we see how these complex cultural relationships and values are intertwined with power, we assume more responsibilities for the cultural influences of our pasts, and begin to live our cultural futures more fully.

These views of the importance of culture and power are based partly on a social intelligence principle that we are social beings, due to the fact that learning cultures helps us to survive and navigate our lives. Because we are taught what cultures are, social intelligence helps us to understand how our cultures continue to affect whatever we do. Even though we may resist changing our own cultural socialization, social intelligence clarifies our visions of what is possible for ourselves and others, and motivates us to persist in our efforts to formulate our own goals, given the continuously demanding challenges of our cultures and their power.

By deliberately unlearning and relearning our cultures, we choose what it is that we want to learn. As adults we are more in charge of our individual and social destinies than we were as children, and social intelligence—or emotional maturity—results from the new value choices that we make, given our broader vision of social realities, and our increased steadfastness in accomplishing social justice. For example, because social intelligence helps us to discern ideals and practices which increase social justice, we may use social intelligence to guide us in learning about other people's cultures as well as our own, so that we increase our understanding and appreciation of social diversity. Furthermore, when we decide to increase even just one of our cherished values, such as education, we will also eventually increase social justice. Thus, we contribute to the common good when we increase our awareness of the strength of cultural influences in our behavior and in social intelligence.

An effective way to increase our social intelligence, through changing our cultural values, is to conduct ourselves differently in our families. When we want to increase the importance we give to education, for example, we need first to find ways to educate ourselves. Our new direction may include assessing opportunities for both formal education, such as gaining a particular credential for professional improvement, and informal education, such as reading serious newspapers or developing more effective study habits. Having a goal of valuing education deepens our understanding of how our families respect or do not respect education, and of how we and our children make commitments to learn.

Culture is ultimately connected with power both in our families and in societies. Social intelligence helps us to recognize more of the subtleties of these connections, so that we do not pursue relatively meaningless goals, like upward social mobility, for a lifetime. We need to develop more substantial missions for our life works, so that we can truly be our own selves and make more adequate contributions to the common good and social justice.

VI. What Difference Does Social Intelligence Make?

Society and History

The fifth and last strand of social intelligence is society itself, sometimes more appropriately thought of as history or globalization. Societal dimensions of our social being are crucial to understanding our families. We become more socially intelligent when we see the broader pictures of our lives and our families more accurately, and when we put our family issues and problems in societal contexts such as history or globalization.

One of the differences that social intelligence makes is that we become historical actors—as individuals, families, groups, or societies. Being able to think of ourselves as members of societies strengthens our senses of being connected to historical forces, and makes us more aware of who we are from the point of view of historical changes and globalization. When we think for ourselves in this way, we can more easily choose the extent to which we go with the flow of history, or stand counter to some contemporary trends.

Historical currents of family trends in modern times, which influence all families, include people marrying at older ages, larger numbers of small families, greater varieties of family types, continuing fragmentations of families through geographical migrations or divorces, increased rifts between nuclear families and their extended kin, decreases in the significance of family elders, the relative dominance of members of the younger generations, increases in single parent families, increases in two career or dual-earning families, and tendencies to delay child-bearing. Although many of us believe that our decision-making around these major family issues expresses only our individual preferences or personal tendencies, this view is not as constructive as trying to assess the varied impacts that national or global trends have on our thinking and behavior. Even though our family choices are not determined by societal trends, we may need to actively resist them, in order to make more independent decisions. Being alert to family trends in society helps us to be more adequately informed when we make family decisions.

Social intelligence, based on societal perspectives, highlights the competing values and lifestyles of families in different cultures within and among societies. Even though there are myriad cultural variants of family behavior, there are also many shared basic family needs that must be fulfilled, so that we can provide family members with sufficient stability and emotional satisfaction.

Deliberately cultivating social intelligence not only increases our appreciation of cultural diversity among families, but also helps us to assess the extent to which we are influenced by broad social trends. For example, we are often strongly influenced by social pressures to conform to others, without realizing the impact that conformity has on us. However, our greater emotional freedom and higher level of autonomy, which result from our increased social intelligence, make us more resistant to pressures to conform to others' expectations. Our increased immunity to social pressures to conform enables us to consider our own interests more fully and more accurately.

Societal perspectives in social intelligence give us some of the broadest social contexts for our thinking. This fifth dimension of social intelligence provides ways to assess the impacts of the other four dimensions of social intelligence: families, beliefs, social classes, and cultures. Because social intelligence is multifaceted, we can assess the impact of families, beliefs, social classes, cultures, and societies in any given social situation.

Being socially intelligent means that we think through what we are going to do from the points of views of the different social systems of families, beliefs, social classes, cultures, and societies. When we develop habits of thought which are based on these particular social systems, we are not only more socially intelligent, but also more enlightened in our decision-making, and in the actions we take in our families and in other social settings.

Historical perspectives on families are particularly valuable in any consideration of societal influences on families. Historical information deepens our appreciation of the evolution of our families, as well as of the most basic needs that families have met through time. Even though there are wide variations in our historical and global patterns of companionship or sexual orientation within families, abiding needs for protection and nurture sharpen our ideas about the extent to which all families share basic emotional concerns about our survival and extinction.

Our families survive or perish partly as consequences of our innate fight or flight tendencies, which are also influenced by our shared values and social pressures. It may appear that because families are one of our earliest historical and evolutionary forms of social life, they are here to stay. However, a case can also be made that families' social and emotional foundations need to be better understood, through social intelligence, if we are to survive, thrive, and live meaningfully in our families during these complex modern times.

Social Justice

When increasing our social intelligence becomes a deliberate way of personal or professional life, our syntheses of concerns about the social influences of families, beliefs, social classes, cultures, and societies also become more coherent. We begin to recognize the subtle differences between going about our daily lives without systematic thought or reflection, and living with the guidance of our new awareness about social intelligence. However, using social intelligence does not consistently make our lives easier, as much as it adds significance and meaning to our daily routines. Social intelligence makes us more observant, keeps us awake to increased possibilities, and ultimately relieves family tensions.

In part it is an ethical issue to raise the question of "So what?" when considering the differences that social intelligence makes. What are the purposes and benefits of letting social intelligence guide our lives? Why should we care about having any direction, purpose, or momentum as we go about our daily chores? One answer to these questions is that we get our act together more efficiently and more effectively when we pay sufficient attention to the social influences of our families, beliefs, social classes, cultures, and societies in our everyday lives.

We also become more integrated within ourselves, and in relation to others, when we increase our social intelligence. At the same time, we stand more firmly on our own ground, and are more able to act autonomously and independently, when we use social intelligence to guide our actions. In some respects, learning directly about social intelligence is a meaningful short cut to being able to live in very purposeful and desirable ways. For example, when we decide what it means for us to have a career that increases social justice, we can use social intelligence to formulate clearer directions for our efforts and energies.

Once we realize that the difference that social intelligence makes in our lives is that we become stronger, and more able to increase life-satisfaction for ourselves and our families, we become more motivated to cultivate social intelligence for its own sake. However, because we necessarily live in series of complex social situations, one way out of these continued pressures may be to choose goals which transcend the pettiness of our immediate desires. We must go beyond meeting our own needs if we are to live fully, according to the vision of social intelligence.

One of the quickest ways to get out of our self-centered neediness is to look toward the ideal of social justice. Social justice orients us toward developing social conditions in families, groups, and societies that allow other people to become socially intelligent.

A practical starting point for pursuing the goal of social justice in particular social contexts is to apply it in our own families. This is a significant beginning because those emotionally closest to us are interested in our survival and fulfillment, and it is easier for us to act on behalf of relatives who share our heritage and concerns. It is also safer for us to try to apply social justice in our own families than in other groups, because we are not as predictably shunned by our families if our efforts to apply social intelligence cause some discomfort, some discontent, or backfire.

Understanding ourselves through the prisms of social intelligence and our own families makes us different. When we develop social intelligence we broaden our interests and needs, and sooner or later make at least some intellectual connections between social intelligence and social justice. When we understand these links, we can create or design what might be possible in our families and in our societies, at the same time realizing that when we continue to cultivate social intelligence, we indirectly pursue social justice. The practical knowledge we gain from social intelligence gradually suggests ways to increase enlightenment and social justice.

Working toward social justice does not begin and end with applications to our own families, although addressing our family needs continues to be both a concern and a responsibility. Ultimately social justice requires us to take our learning about our families into broader arenas. We become socially intelligent about our families not only to improve our own families according to the ideals and principles of social justice, but also in order to think more clearly about societies' needs, and to work toward increasing the common good. A morally responsible life is not based solely on meeting our own interests, or on creating optimal conditions for our families, but in addition is engaged with increasing opportunities for less fortunate members of societies. Both social intelligence and social justice help us to make wiser choices about how to bring about a better world.

VII. How Do We See Families Differently?

Social intelligence enables us to see ourselves and our families differently. This ability to see beyond conventional interpretations of social realities is based on our awareness of the impacts of the five dimensions of social intelligence on our lives: families, beliefs, social classes, cultures, and societies. When we observe and assess the effects of these five major social influences in different situations, we identify the power and significance of social pressures more accurately, as well as understand the systemic relationships among families, beliefs, social classes, cultures, and societies more fully.

Social intelligence also requires that we see social realities that extend beyond the time and place of our specific present situations. A socially intelligent vision of what is, and what could be, is influenced by both history and cross cultural comparisons. When we broaden our points of reference, we see beyond the immediacy of present problem dimensions, and find clues about how to solve these issues by seeing the existing pressures in broader social contexts. For example, stresses in contemporary families may in large part be related to the pervasive lack of kin presence and support, rather than to any particular personality characteristics of nuclear family members. Seeing the global realities of kin in many other families enables us to appreciate the functions that extended family members fill, as well as the continuities that are still needed in today's contemporary families.

Families and Social Intelligence

Comparing what families look like today, with broad historical and global family conditions, deepens our understanding of families in their own right, as well as provides us with more realistic views of family possibilities. For example, tendencies to expect a great deal from personal relationships and companionship in contemporary families blot out the fact that these expectations and values are relatively recent developments, and that families have existed for generations with alternative, perhaps more practical, or more functional bases for personal and intimate relationships. Thus, when we use broader perspectives to understand our current family problems, we develop new ideals and new goals about how to achieve more satisfactory family relationships.

In general, whatever we see in our lives depends on our understanding and our experiences. Education and learning change our perceptions, and building practical social knowledge—an integral part of increasing our social intelligence—gives us a new view of our recurring or most troublesome family problems. An advantage of seeing things differently, through social intelligence, is that we can more easily create new strategies to change ourselves and our families. Because our current social realities are based on a variety of interlocking social systems, as well as on families, when we see and do things differently in our families, ripple effects from our actions are experienced in social systems as well as in families.

In order to change ourselves, our families, or our societies, we must first have ideas of what these changes could be. Although our visions of these possibilities may not be clear or precise, our new views sharpen as we collect information about particular family or social problems and conditions. In order to change ourselves or our families, we have to see different modes of being or relationships, for example, so that we can proceed with actually making these changes based on our social intelligence.

Sometimes our understanding of the social conditions of our families is sketchy, especially when we try to account for historical or cross-cultural family experiences and family contrasts. However, being aware of patterns in these broader trends is sufficient to prepare us to move forward with new visions and new ideas. When we continue to make in-depth learning about our families a valued goal, we stay open to benefiting from finding more facts whenever opportunities arise.

Our ways of seeing our families need to be more influenced by the information and facts we find out about families, especially about our own families, than by our feelings and emotions about our families. Trying to analyze and understand family feelings and sentiments accurately is extremely difficult and problematic, because we could analyze our feelings and sentiments indefinitely. This process drains our energies more than trying to understand the major events or turning points in our families' histories, which in the long run yield more significant information. Furthermore, collecting facts about our families, rather than labeling feelings or sentiments, has the effect of toning down some of our emotional reactivity, so that we can decide more easily what needs to be done—for individuals, families, and societies—to bring about particular changes.

As we begin to see our families differently, we necessarily define our freedom and responsibilities in our families differently. Keeping our attention on family facts enables us to identify the impairing effects of some emotions in our families, and increasing our social intelligence about destructive emotions strengthens our immunity to them. Both our present and our future families benefit from our increased social intelligence, which enables us not only to see our families differently, but also to act differently in our families and in society.

Vision and Precision

Our eyes direct us when we walk and go about our everyday business, in the same way that our vision of things past, present, and future directs our behavior. Because we must imagine possibilities before they become realities, for example, we need to create coherent visions of what we want to accomplish, in order to make viable changes in our families and in societies. Throughout these processes we also visualize ourselves, either deliberately or unconsciously, so that we become our own self-fulfilling prophecies in action.

Social intelligence is a tool which helps us to build practical knowledge that enhances the effectiveness of our actions in our families, as well as in other social settings. Following our best understanding of families, beliefs, social classes, cultures, and societies we observe social realities more accurately, think more clearly, and imagine more precisely. Sometimes, however, our abilities to formulate visions of what could be, and the precision we employ to do this, may not seem to be sufficient. For example, we may have only vague ideas that something in our families needs to be changed, without being sure what this is. However, if we essentially take leaps of faith, as we move in the general directions of family balance or social justice, we ultimately clarify our specific goals.

When we have more adequate reserves of social intelligence to direct our behavior, our families become more constructive arenas as we implement gradual and responsible changes to improve family functioning and family relationships. Although our families frequently resist our efforts to accomplish changes, when we modify our own behavior—by using social intelligence to guide our interactions with family members—we initiate shifts in family patterns that ultimately change our families' emotional systems. However, we need to be particularly cautious in using social intelligence to intervene in social settings that are less tenacious than our families. If we try to accomplish these same kinds of changes in our work systems, or among our friends, for example, our efforts may all too easily backfire, so that we find ourselves without a job or without friends.

Our efforts to accomplish changes in our families should be informed by the broad perspectives of social intelligence, if we are to envision realistic possibilities, as well as sufficiently accurate options. Although we cannot predict precisely what our relatives' responses will be to our particular moves, social intelligence helps us to deal with others' negative reactions or intense resistance. Even though what we want to accomplish is to enhance our most constructive personal talents and intentions—for example, to be a stronger person who makes more socially intelligent decisions—family members predictably pressure us to return to our former ways of doing things. When the equilibrium and balance of our family emotional systems is upset, relatives who did not initiate the changes will usually resist, or temporarily reject, the vision and precision communicated by the person or persons making the changes.

Seeing ourselves and our families differently through social intelligence is a tricky business. Our changed perceptions lead us in directions of wanting to heal or improve ourselves and our family relationships, and yet these efforts are predictably resisted by other family members. Even when we labor to formulate a vision of new possibilities for change, and add precision to our vision of these possibilities through increasing our social intelligence, we may still meet with relatives' resistance at every turn.

Strategies which ease our relatives' discomfort in accepting new patterns of family interaction include being gently but responsibly persistent in our enlightened efforts, as well as continuing to inform our actions through gathering as many social facts as possible. We achieve this by understanding the social dimensions and histories of our families, as well as the broader trends and patterns of families in our own localities, religions, social classes, cultures, and societies. Thus social intelligence enables us to be more empathic in understanding our families' reactions, and more responsible in designing our change strategies.

Social intelligence is the continuing, most reliable source of our vision and precision about our families. In order to keep our vision and precision about these emotional, complex relationship systems clear, we need to learn more about the broader social systems that affect us. The increased social intelligence, which this knowledge provides, becomes part of us when we apply it in our everyday thinking and behavior. Our clearer, more precise vision helps us to act more responsibly, as well as to accomplish more of what we want for ourselves, our families, our communities, and our societies.

History and Patterns

The history that many of us learned in school tended to be political, national, and linear. We frequently learned how national events unfolded through time, for example, and how the most powerful groups in our societies challenged our governments. In modern times, international analyses are included with national histories, especially when international wars are increasingly significant parts of our national histories.

We have been late to recognize the importance of social history, which is more grounded in events and changes that take place among lower class populations, than is customary in conventional political histories. Even though there have been more attempts to link social history and political history in recent years, there are still strong tendencies to divide local and national histories. By contrast social intelligence makes focused efforts to link family histories with local, national, and global histories. Because the thinking necessary to do this is easily burdened with detailed or inaccurate information, a helpful research strategy is to identify repetitions in patterns of behavior in these complex historical and social influences.

One of the most important first steps, toward successfully increasing the social intelligence of groups and individuals, is to recognize dominant patterns of behavior that repeat themselves amidst complex historical and social influences. When we consider family trends, for example, we should identify ways in which families are fragmented or held together. We also need to find patterns in international aspects of global events, such as wars, and in broad social processes, such as migrations and family traditions. Furthermore, finding recurring sequences in both individual and collective actions in these broad arenas is an accurate, practical approach to articulating real connections among these complex influences.

When we recognize historical trends, and add family or social patterns in these contexts, we increase our social intelligence. We need to think historically in order to achieve sufficient depth in our understanding of how social influences impact our families. In fact, we understand history more fully by identifying social influences that affect us and our families the most. For example, wars should not be considered only from the viewpoints of governments or military personnel: official military histories do not stand alone as reliable sources of knowledge about wars. They need to be supplemented by accounts of sacrifices made, or anguish experienced, by both military troops and their families. Thus, official military history perspectives are put in more accurate historical and social contexts, when we consider reports by individuals and families directly involved in wars.

Reviewing biographies is another useful way to link personal experiences, especially in families, to broad historical trends. Unfortunately many biographies include information about historical circumstances as incidental background material in describing selected life experiences, rather than as solid points of departure for understanding and explaining these lives. Social intelligence emphasizes that history is much more significant than a mere background of relatively unimportant or random events. History is consequential for us all, and may assume causal significance in understanding important aspects of ourselves and our families.

We increase our social intelligence by collecting biographical information about members of our families. These data make national or global histories come alive, as well as help us to see social and historical trends and conditions that made significant differences to us, our relatives, and our ancestors. Oral accounts of the immediate past are invaluable unique resources, for example, even though this information may not be remembered accurately. Oral histories are valuable because they are based on lived experiences, and they usually explicitly combine information about family interactions with selective knowledge of national and global social influences.

Family stories about dramas of emigration and immigration, although not precise, also give meaningful foundations to more intellectually-oriented national and international histories. In order to understand our families, we need to know which of our relatives were left behind by our families' migrants, for example, and which of our family migrants ultimately prospered. These facts suggest significant patterns of family behavior that ultimately lead toward our survival or extinction.

History, as well as patterns of behavior which help us to understand history's influences on our families, are much more than evidence of past behavior. In order to be socially intelligent, we must extend the meanings of history to our contemporary everyday lives. We can identify, for example, which patterns of behavior in our families and in societies increased the constructive impacts that historical trends had, and may continue to have, on our families. Social intelligence requires the cultivation of historical awareness, which includes considering many complex influences and patterns of behavior. One of our socially intelligent goals is to become historical actors, so that we ourselves can affect continuing historical and social processes.

Facts Not Feelings

Both family histories and patterns of behavior in families involve events and relationships based on facts. As human beings we also have feelings about family events, relationships, or facts. However, from the point of view of social intelligence, we learn best about ourselves, our families, and other families when we scrutinize facts rather than feelings. Putting together factual histories of our families frequently cools our feelings about these facts, so that although our feelings are not eliminated by creating or focusing on our family histories, they are made more manageable.

Patterns of family behavior are also often associated with major family events like a job change, a birth, a loss, or a geographical separation. Patterns of behavior develop around the facts of these significant family changes, in order to adapt to the shifts that occurred, and in order to ritualize some of the feelings around the events. When we either develop behaviors, or practice rituals, to deal with major family events, we bring both facts and feelings associated with the events more under our control. For example, at a time of family loss, we depend on grieving and funeral rituals to heal and support us as we mourn.

An important key to understanding particular feelings is to discover the family events and facts that underlie the evocation and sustenance of our strongest feelings. We experience anger, for example, when we are manipulated by other family members, and we may discover that these manipulations usually occur during major family events, such as the loss of a parent, a parent's loss of a close relative, a child leaving home as a young adult, or a sibling losing a job.

Paying close attention to the facts of our families' conditions provides valuable information about our most problematic family dependencies, and consequently increases our social intelligence. Once we have identified that dysfunctional repetitions in family behavior follow particular events, for example, we can use social intelligence to design strategies to deal with these problems. The problem-solving potential of social intelligence works more effectively from bases of information and facts, than from analyses of feelings and emotions experienced in problem situations.

When we gather facts, from observing our families, or from asking other relatives about particular family events, we define our family situations more clearly. By contrast, when we concentrate on identifying our most powerful feelings or emotions, and on analyzing these in the context of our family relationships, we tend to increase our negative feelings, as well as feel increasingly powerless over them. In sum, focusing on our feelings and emotions increases their relatively limitless power to harm us and our families. Becoming overwhelmed by our feelings and emotions is counterproductive to solving family problems, and serves no real purpose beyond allowing us to realize the depths of our sentiments about ourselves and our family problems.

Social intelligence gives us new views of our families because emphasizing family facts, rather than feelings, helps us to build meaningful family histories. When we realize that our families are emotional systems, and that our emotions are magnified or diminished by specific patterns of behavior, we understand why the intensity of our families' emotions varies through time. Looking at information about past generations of our families, for example, gives us clues about how our families have continued to hold together in spite of their losses and migrations. We can ask significant questions like who were the major survivors of our past family emotional systems? Who were the victims, perhaps dying as children, in these complex social and emotional processes? To what extent do some of these past patterns of behavior repeat in current generations? What does it take to survive in our families today, rather than succumb to the destructive influences of their emotional systems?

Social intelligence does not ignore or deny family feelings and emotions, but rather encourages explorations of feelings and emotions through the facts of important family events, as well as through the facts of family adaptations to major historical or relationship events. We become researchers of our families when we collect information about emotionally significant facts, and we inevitably see our families differently as a consequence. If we maintain sufficient objectivity about our family emotional systems, we increase our social intelligence, and decrease our vulnerability to negative family emotions.

Freedom and Responsibility

Conventionally speaking families are usually thought of as sites of serious responsibilities, rather than arenas of freedom. Social intelligence presents some different views and priorities for consideration, assuming that we are interested in the long term balance and durability of our families. A social systems model of family interactions is based on the idea that individual family members function optimally when they are autonomous or free. At the same time, however, social intelligence draws attention to the fact that family freedom needs to be used for the betterment of others, as well as for the fulfillment of personal goals.

As we venture forth in our explorations of social intelligence in our families, we examine both social conditions that are conducive to the freedom of family members within our families and in societies, and social conditions that make it possible for family members to be responsible within our families and in society. Social intelligence requires us to consider conditions outside our families as well as within them, while we continue to act on our assessments of social influences related to our families, beliefs, social classes, cultures, and societies.

Freedom in our families and societies is essentially the capacity to think clearly, and to act toward goals which empower self and increase the common good. Freedom is not an idea or ideal which is devoid of social relationships and social influences, but rather it infers particular ways of operating in families and societies. Freedom does not mean that we act completely independently or randomly, but rather in responsible relation to our families, communities, and societies.

Responsibility in our families and societies is also based on our capacities to think clearly, and to act toward goals which empower self and increase the common good. This means that a sound working definition of responsibility is virtually the same as the one given for the idea and ideal of freedom. Thus social intelligence reduces the polarizations and conflicts evoked by more popular, conventional definitions of freedom and responsibility, which see freedom and responsibility as mutually exclusive: we are free only when we do not have responsibilities. Furthermore, when we deepen our understanding of how major social influences either threaten our well-being, or work well for us, we see closer relationships between freedom and responsibility.

Families and Social Intelligence

Although many of us fear our families, because they seem never-ending in their demands on our time and energy, we may at the same time have deep yearnings to behave responsibly, and to contribute to the common good through our families and societies. Social intelligence helps us to see that when we consider freedom and responsibility more broadly, we do not have to sacrifice our freedom in order to be responsible. Rather, being responsible is a significant aspect of our freedom, especially when we consider the social conditions which are necessary for the freedom of others as well as ourselves.

Social intelligence shows us the extent to which we are dependent on others for our well-being, most particularly on our families. For example, we depend on our families for our security—emotional, financial, and historical. In fact, it is only when we honor our deepest connections to our families that we become sufficiently free to do what we need to do, as well as more responsible for creating and maintaining these conditions of freedom for ourselves and others.

The greater breadth of vision about our families, which we gain from increasing our social intelligence, is one of the optimal conditions for preserving our freedom and taking responsibility in our families and societies. When we see that our well-being, security, and roots are connected to our societies as well as to our families, we realize that it is imperative to strengthen our broad social connections, as well as our family bonds. As we teach our children and grandchildren about life, we cannot confine our views to our families. We need to orient members of our youngest generations to exercise their freedom and responsibilities in societies as well as in their families.

Social intelligence shows that freedom and responsibility have some differences as well as similarities in their overlapping goals and ideals. Freedom starts within families for both children and adults, for example, and it is only when freedom is a well-defined pattern of interaction within families that the most constructive responsibilities for families and societies can flow from that freedom. In order to be responsible in our families and society, we must first be free. Freedom is a practical precondition of responsibility, and social intelligence enables us to see the meaningful interdependence of these ideals, and to establish family and societal freedom.

Seeing Emotions

Social intelligence is based on the principle that it is helpful to see and understand our families as emotional systems. Examining the emotional systems of our families reveals the major social forces which underlie their patterns of interaction, and this is significant because our families orient us to ourselves and the world. Sometimes, however, it is difficult to identify the emotional systems in our families, because emotions and emotional reactivity have many different forms and processes.

Emotions hold families together, albeit frequently in relationships that are too close for comfort. When family emotional systems exclude outsiders, or shun family members, the closure of these emotional systems heightens the emotional dependency and intensity in their relationships. Closed emotional systems are rigid and tend to fragment, frequently resulting in dysfunctional families. Although it is easier to see the workings of closed rather than open emotional systems, because closed emotional systems have more intense emotions and dependencies, closed families engender the most serious family problems. There is less freedom, and therefore reduced capacities and inclinations to assume responsibilities for actions and outcomes, in families with closed emotional systems.

Closed family emotional systems have ritualized relationships, which are both emotionally distant and emotionally reactive. Repeated patterns of behavior in these families are relatives' attempts to control their uncomfortable emotions. However, the apparent absence of conventional sentimental expressions in closed family relationships does not mean that their relationships are devoid of emotions. Rather, emotional distance is sometimes a desperately contrived attempt to cope with difficult-to-manage emotions.

Emotions are more dramatic, and more marked, in families which tend to be closed and dysfunctional. Social intelligence helps us to discern imbalances in patterns of family interaction, so that we can begin to know where appropriate adaptations and other changes can be made. In order to increase our objectivity about our families, we should observe their emotions closely, collect facts about patterns in family functioning over time, and assess the lifetime trajectories of older and deceased generations of family members. These methods help us to see and understand our family histories as emotional systems.

In contrast to closed emotional system families, families with more open emotional systems are more functional and have less obvious patterns in their everyday family interaction. More open families may not overflow with positive emotions, however, as suggested by conventional beliefs about optimal family functioning. Rather, families with open emotional systems are relatively calm, most of the time, with meaningful and appropriate expressions of emotions that flow more or less continuously. For example, open emotional system families express fitting emotions during major turning points such as births, deaths, achievements, losses, illnesses, and other critical family situations. Emotions in open families are not explosive or extreme, but rather make their families work well.

Open families provide secure emotional roots for their family members, rather than generate restrictive routines or inhibit actions as in closed families. Emotions in open families yield more elastic family relationships, which enable their family members to come and go with ease, and provide needed support to members of the youngest and oldest generations. Divisions of labor in open family emotional systems are more balanced, so that no single family members become overly burdened, or crippled, by family responsibilities and chores.

The contrasts in closed and open emotional systems in families help us to identify the emotional conditions that exist in our own families, as well as conditions that would be optimal. When we see problematic dimensions of family emotional systems, we deepen and broaden our perspectives on these issues, so that we change our own behavior, or find strategies to resolve emotional imbalances. Seeing emotions in families facilitates movement in these constructive directions, and the ideal of social justice makes us aware of the problems and needs of other families as well as our own.

Social intelligence clarifies our priorities. It is all too easy to dismiss the importance of emotions in our families, especially when they go beyond the stereotypes of romantic love, or child-care, which we associate with modern families. We need to recognize that emotions can be dangerous or lethal to family members, in order to be more objective about the emotions that rule our lives.

When we are children, we frequently feel restricted by our parents' discipline, but as adults we may also allow parental influences to dictate our life choices. Although this extension of the power of the emotional systems of our families may not be readily apparent, we need to scrutinize the emotional systems of our families in order to see and understand what is really going on. Have we actually taken charge of our own lives, or are we still trying to earn parental approval? Do we think for ourselves, or do we follow lines of parental preferences in our reasoning? Do we let family expectations define how we parent our children or conduct our daily lives?

Building for Tomorrow

When we see complexities in the inner workings of our families, as well as assess impacts of social influences on our families, we become historical actors with concerns for the future, as well as for the past and present. However, we also need to be sure that we consider global perspectives, in addition to local and national perspectives, in this venture.

Our social intelligence, as well as developing interests in social justice, leads us to ask ourselves what sort of world we want to build for tomorrow. Because we have free choices, albeit within some physiological and social constraints, we can consider and create responsible visions of worlds that would be both more productive and more benign, and of families that launch their young adults successfully into such worlds.

Families and Social Intelligence

Social intelligence is a distillation of knowledge about five powerful social influences that make visible and tangible differences in our lives: families, beliefs, social classes, cultures, and societies. Families are our anchors or foundations for varied kinds of social participation, so we need to be aware of the events and processes that emerge or repeat in our kin groups. In many important respects our families are our grand opportunities to bring the world of tomorrow to fruition: it is easier to change ourselves and our families than it is to have significant impacts on societies.

When we look toward the future, if only at the immediate future, we need to assess to what extent our decisions increase freedom and social justice. We also need to ask how we can bring long term perspectives to what we do, so that we plan not only for our own family needs, but also for broader social realities. In addition, how can we most effectively communicate, to members of the younger generations of our families, what it is that we have learned about ourselves, and the world, that will protect and nurture them?

Our most significant statements of purpose are made through our actions rather than through our words. For example, we should do today whatever it takes to build a better world for tomorrow. Social intelligence shows us that people often resist or resent being advised about the future, especially as it is viewed as presumptuous to suggest answers to tomorrow's problems. However, learning and teaching our family members about how to increase our social intelligence helps us to be prepared for whatever happens in an unpredictable future.

The five dimensions of social intelligence—families, beliefs, social classes, cultures, and societies—enable us to see these significant social realities in broad contexts, with the result that we become more informed in our decision-making and actions. When we act according to social intelligence, and these particular perspectives, we are more enlightened in our decision-making for the future, as well as for the present. Aligning ourselves with these five major social influences strengthens our immunity to their possible destructiveness. If, by contrast, we act automatically, without deliberate thought, there are real dangers that these five powerful social influences will take over our lives and limit, rather than increase, our freedom.

It is much easier for people not to think about social intelligence at all, and to coast along, trusting that the best will happen. To a certain extent this is a viable life option, because we are often protected by our own adequate socialization. For example, many of us were taught to look after our own interests, and this orientation may serve us for a lifetime. However, sooner or later we need to at least consider whether this is the best way to conduct ourselves, given our observations and experiences of the world's considerable pain and tragedies. Questions inevitably emerge about how we can harvest more human potential. Also, how can people be fulfilled, rather than merely survive or struggle with life-threatening social conditions?

Seeing who we are, as well as what we can do with social intelligence, answers some of these questions. We lead quite different lives when we see our situations through lenses of social intelligence, and we transmit our new visions to others when we live according to these principles. Our families are fundamentally important in accomplishing these changes, and we need to continue to interact with our families differently if we are to build a better world for tomorrow.

VIII. How Do We Interact With Families Differently?

Social intelligence is a principle of action. It is important not only to see our families differently, but also to know how to interact with them differently. First it is important to respect our families as the longest-existing social institution in society. Families perform functions necessary to meet our collective needs for survival—the foundation for our ultimate fulfillment. Next we have to recognize the emotional power that our families wield over us, for better or for worse, so that any actions we take have unavoidable repercussions for others as well as for ourselves.

For these reasons we need to approach our families with considerable caution and awe, before making even slight changes in how we relate to them day by day. Social intelligence suggests, for example, that we should move ahead with plans for moderate changes in what we do, only if we are truly observant and knowledgeable about the emotional reactivity our actions will provoke, and only if we have the capacity and willingness to make further changes in our actions when needed. We exercise such caution because our families should not suffer from our actions, however well-intentioned we are, or however well-informed and enlightened we think we are through using social intelligence.

One of the most important premises of social intelligence is that social systems, particularly families, become reactive and resist innovation whenever changes are initiated, and especially when changes are pushed upon them. Therefore, when deliberately guiding our actions through social intelligence, we must be prepared for these responses. When we first try to open up our family emotional systems, for example, we need to neutralize some of our relatives' reactive resistance. Furthermore, at the same time, we also need to encourage and nurture our family members' willingness to bring about constructive changes.

This is not to say that we need to wait endlessly for others' approval before we change ourselves or our families. But rather that we should earn some respect for, or compliance with our plans, before making decisive moves. We cannot successfully or ethically force our views on others, and coercive actions are inappropriate.

Once we manage to open up our family systems, we are in stronger positions to move ahead with more changes, relatively regardless of what other family members think or do. If we make bold moves, however, social intelligence cautions us to expect additional resistance and pressure to undo our acts from emotionally significant others. However, knowing that these responses from relatives are predictable makes our new directions easier to accomplish.

Social intelligence also suggests that we will eventually accomplish the changes we want if we are patient in maintaining or adapting our strategies. To do this we should sustain our controversial stands, in spite of others' pressure to return to how things were previously. Persisting in making the changes we deem necessary, and proceeding with care and caution, help us to accomplish these changes in due course. Our respect for others, in these complex change processes, is ultimately transformed into respect or acceptance from others for the difficult task of initiating and achieving constructive changes in our families.

We interact with our families differently when we use the broad perspectives of social intelligence, because we see our relatives in new ways, and because we are motivated to move toward the betterment of our families and humankind. We proceed cautiously and respectfully, because social intelligence makes us more aware of some of the powerful qualities of families and social systems, and we are responsible for any hurt or disruption that our actions may bring.

If our families change too quickly, or if there is too much resistance to the changes we want to make, they may break up, or single out vulnerable family members to become scapegoated victims in the change processes. Because these problematic family behaviors are unintended consequences, rather than deliberately initiated changes, they should be avoided if possible. Social intelligence makes us more responsible, because we can better anticipate the consequences of our actions, which requires us to be supremely cautious in initiating changes in ourselves and in our families.

Dramatic spontaneous changes in our families are most easily seen around family crises like the death of an emotionally significant family member. Families are not only disoriented by their grief for the lost relative at this time, but they may also become completely disorganized or reorganized. Although making deliberate changes in our families does not usually precipitate such extreme upheavals, social intelligence helps us to recognize families' capacities to change their relationship systems overnight in crisis situations, and to understand more fully the considerable dimensions and possibilities of family changes. Although we cannot know specific details about our families' reactivity to our considered changes in advance, we can recognize how family emotional systems predictably react negatively to their members' efforts to initiate changes.

Action as Responsibility

Social intelligence is a cognitive tool, a concept, a synthesis of perspectives, a hypothesis, and a tentative theory which describes and explains intellectual, social, and emotional processes. Social intelligence is also a powerful acquired capacity, a series of experiences, a sequence of acts and behaviors based on social facts, enlightenment, and social justice. Social intelligence is action research; an everyday means to accomplish individual, family and social changes; and an ideal or goal that influences personal, professional, collective, and social priorities.

Controlling our social intelligence—increasing it, or letting it stagnate below the level of our consciousness—is a choice we make. When we attain a basic understanding of social intelligence, we should decide whether we want to consider or ignore social intelligence as we go about our daily lives. We can also decide to call upon social intelligence either occasionally or continuously. However, until we experience some of the differences between living with or without the guidance of social intelligence, we cannot fully appreciate the seriousness of the consequences of making decisions for or against using social intelligence.

This presents a paradox. We may need to use social intelligence before we can really understand it. Also, we need to experiment to some extent, by trial and error, until we get a clearer sense of how our thinking changes when we look at situations from the points of view of social intelligence. Once we see things differently, we act differently. Furthermore, as we become more aware of the changes that thinking and acting with social intelligence make, we begin to consider social justice more seriously. When this happens, responsible action becomes a stronger prioritizing influence in our decision-making and behavior.

In any event, even if our interest in social intelligence originates as a practical or an intellectual pursuit, sooner or later we have to use social intelligence in our own day-by-day lives, if these basic ideas and principles are to be fully understood. When we apply social intelligence to our families, for example, we have to understand the different roles we play—son, daughter, father, mother, grandfather, grandmother—from the points of view of our family emotional systems and varied social systems. This will make us more aware of the power of dependence and independence in our families, as well as allow us to appreciate the influences of societies and history. These contrasting views inform how we act in our families, to the extent that we are open and receptive to the new perspectives. We become more responsible when we deepen our understanding of what social intelligence is. We also become more responsible when we use social intelligence to become more aware of the social dimensions of our situations, so that we make the wisest decisions we can, as well as take optimal courses of action. Social intelligence encourages us to become more responsible for our families' well-being, because of the importance of dependency needs in our families, as well as for some aspects of social justice in society.

Responsible action in our families includes telling the truth as we see it, and working toward enabling all family members to be strong. We have responsibilities to stop exploitation and abuse in our families, by interacting with our relatives in socially intelligent ways. This often includes supporting victimized family members, and trying to reduce the power and influence of dominant family members. Our actions can be radical or gradual, depending on our family members' receptiveness and readiness for change. Outside assistance is sometimes necessary, and socially intelligent family members will need to strategize about how to choose appropriate community supports and resources for additional guidance and interventions when necessary.

It is often difficult to be sufficiently objective to act as effective change agents in our families. In this situation, external community and professional advice should be called upon, to increase our objectivity and social intelligence, in order to cope with our dysfunctional or imbalanced family relationships. However, we must not stay solely focused on these problematic aspects of our families' interactions. The lack of objectivity we necessarily have about our own family situations will eventually contradict the more socially intelligent advantages of the breadth of vision we gain from understanding the influences of other families, beliefs, social classes, cultures, and societies on our families' problems. In order to be fully responsible in our uses of social intelligence, we need to make sure that our actions continue to be guided by such broad perspectives and social systems, as well as by our particular family needs.

Action and the Risks

There are several risks involved in either using or not using social intelligence as a guide to taking action in our families. Because we necessarily develop some social intelligence when we are socialized and oriented to life by our parents and relatives, it is logical to ask why we need more. For example, who really enjoys being watchful about the effects of the influences of families, beliefs, social classes, cultures, and societies in our daily behavior? Do we risk not having fun and enjoyment when we do this? Do we short-change ourselves when we wrestle with just some of the serious questions that social intelligence poses? All in all, however, even though developing social intelligence involves real and difficult challenges, the social influences and social complexities we encounter daily are so demanding that we need more social intelligence than our families usually give us, in order to be truly independent and effective in our different worlds.

We learn a great deal about society during our schooling, and our teachers are powerful influences in helping us to cultivate broad orientations to self and others. However, because school teaching and formal learning are primarily intellectual rather than practical, we find that we are still in need of reliable pointers in our everyday decision-making. Furthermore, although religions may serve as dependable guides for some people, or for some of our actions, the degree of religious faith needed to make such guidance salient and meaningful is relatively rare, rather than widespread in society, as well as difficult or impossible for many of us to achieve.

Given this void in our available resources, social intelligence can be relatively easily learned, as well as applied to a wide variety of circumstances. When we make social intelligence our own, it becomes a relatively secure way to orient ourselves, and we become more independent rather than dependent in this process. If we are unable to come up with answers to our concerns, for example, we can call upon relatives for more information, or we can get direction from other individuals or groups. Learning about the broad dimensions of social intelligence suggests myriad ways to undo their negative impacts on our actions.

The most useful starting point for increasing our social intelligence is to collect information about how we interact with our families. This task encourages responsible, informed action, as well as reminds us about the expansiveness and meaningfulness of the personal and social issues that move us the most. Increasing our social intelligence in our families ultimately leads us in directions that address the common good in societies, as well as in our families. Thus increasing our social intelligence enables us to act according to our enlightened self interest. At the same time that we maintain our own power, and increase our capacities to relate meaningfully to others, we establish a high priority or ideal to meet others' needs—our relatives and members of societies—through what we do.

Some of the stakes in maintaining these objectives and goals are that we must continue to observe social influences, and take responsible action, or risk having our well-being damaged, as well as that of our families and societies. We cannot function optimally, or adequately, unless we assess and base our actions on the major social influences in our lives. If we ignore our responsibilities, or existential challenges, to act from bases of social intelligence, our lives are narrowed, and we cannot take advantage of the options we would have taken if we had chosen to increase our social intelligence. In brief, refusing to continue to increase our social intelligence restricts our productivity, and prevents us from guiding others effectively toward more expansive goals.

A pervasive social reality is that our families and society are in flux, and that individuals and their families are easily buffeted by the strong social influences of families, beliefs, social classes, cultures, and societies. Unless we stand up to these powers, we are pulled and pushed by their impersonal forces. We become relatively powerless, and often victimized, when we are immersed in negative and contradictory social processes. By contrast, when we keep our attention on deliberately developing social intelligence, we avoid being defined by these strong social influences and their unwanted negative consequences.

Deliberately directing our actions, according to our understanding of social intelligence and social responsibility, makes us more immune to destructive social influences. When we gain a workable degree of control in our lives by increasing our social intelligence, we are less vulnerable to the likelihood that impersonal social forces will drive us to do what we do not want to do, or to become more limited in what we can accomplish. We not only lose our capacities to be free and independent when we run our lives on automatic pilot, but we also evoke unpredictable negative social consequences that are difficult or impossible to handle.

Recognizing Dependency

Another way to gain clarity about our actions is to recognize the intensity of dependencies in our families and other social settings. When we enter into emotionally interdependent relationships, especially in our families, the bonds and connections we establish with others easily become so close that we lose our autonomy. For example, intense family togetherness is maintained by the dependency of individuals in particular relationships and throughout the entire group. This may be such an overwhelming experience, that expressions of individuality are reduced or even obliterated.

Social intelligence is built, in part, upon awareness of the critical importance of tensions between individualities and collectivities. When families, or other groups, have closed relationship systems, for example, their intense dependencies prevent the formation of elastic bonds and open exchanges among their family or group members. One of the ideals of living according to social intelligence is that we try to loosen or open up patterns of tight and rigid dependency, because this ultimately improves all the relationships concerned. When closed emotional systems are opened, freedom, balance, and social justice can develop and increase.

One of the most dramatic examples of the influence of dependency on behavior, which illustrates destructive aspects of dependency, is gang behavior. The conforming, ritualized behavior of gang members leads to a suspension of individual judgment among members, so that group pressures—such as those evoked by the dominance of a leader—take over individuals' abilities to counteract the push and pull of the group. Individuality is essentially lost in these circumstances, and, as a result, the emotional intensity of the gang's unity is easily manipulated by the leader.

Crowd behavior, where perhaps shared panic or political rhetoric takes over individuals' capacities to act in accordance with their own values, is another example of the power of emotional dependency. When we are in continued close proximity with others, individuality may be sacrificed to the will of those who assume dominant positions in the crowd. Perhaps less dramatic, but just as lethal in their consequences, are religious cults or sects where religious leaders take over the capacities of individual members to think for themselves. This extreme kind of religious fundamentalism is similar to political situations, where leaders manipulate crowds and populations with their power and coercive tactics. As in the previous examples, the emotional dependence of followers is exploited, and their freedom is curtailed.

Social intelligence requires us to ask ourselves to what extent conditions and patterns of dependence exist in our families. Even though our family dependencies may not presently be dysfunctional, we need to be alert to this probability, especially in crises such as illness, family conflicts, long term estrangements of particular family members, as well as times of losses or additions such as deaths, births, and family migrations. When the equilibrium of our families is upset, the likelihood of the emergence of problematic patterns of dominance and dependence increases. Paradoxically, these are also times when we can have stronger impacts in resolving past conflicts or estrangements, according to the principles of social intelligence, thereby opening up our family emotional systems.

Social intelligence makes us alert to the dangers of dependence in our own families. When we see family relationships that are primarily based on not rocking the boat, for example, we need to be respectfully suspicious of their dependencies, because they affect the openness or closure of the whole family. Most of all, we need to examine the ways in which we sustain these patterns of dependency ourselves, as well as the ways in which our privileges and advantages are based on other family members' losses of freedom and independence.

Recognizing family dependencies strengthens our abilities to take more socially intelligent actions in our families and society, especially because the characteristics of emotionally reactive family systems are found, to some extent, in other social systems. Dependencies, which restrict access to opportunities to increase well-being, are changed when we find viable ways to loosen them. Because of the difficulty of doing this successfully, without exploiting others, or offending their sensibilities, we need to make sure that we do not contribute directly to problematic dependencies ourselves.

Although all families must meet or cope with the dependency needs of their members, such as those of the young and old, ideally these dependencies do not disrupt the healthy functioning of families. In the long run, especially during times when dependency needs are urgent, families must try to establish conditions that will increase the independence of their family members within their families and in societies. This goal is still a priority when some unavoidable dependency needs— such as physical disability—continue for a lifetime.

Working on Independence

One of our most difficult life tasks is to become independent. Human development studies show that separations

VIII. How Do We Interact With Families Differently?

from parents tend to be extremely difficult when we are young, and that for many of us dependency issues may remain significant long into adulthood and old age. For example, we may find it difficult to think clearly without others' leadership, or to act in accordance with our own thoughts.

A great strength of social intelligence is that it guides us to become more independent. Because human beings are necessarily dependent on each other for protection and survival, becoming independent requires effort and considerable attention. Sometimes however, if we are in danger, or truly need to be accepted by others, going with the flow and conforming to others' expectations may be the most practical short term strategy.

If we decide to conform on a long term basis, letting tradition over-ride our individuality, for example, we may lead comfortable and rewarding lives, but our actions will merely repeat and reinforce what has already been done before us. It is only when we dare to be more independent, and pursue innovative goals, that we become agents of change, as well as participants in the betterment of humankind. Autonomy and freedom allow us to think more clearly, and questioning the status quo creates more opportunities for ourselves and others to have purposeful and fulfilling lives.

When we consider what it means to conform or innovate in our families, we see—and understand through our own experiences—that doing things differently is usually resisted and opposed. When we innovate in our families, by acting according to what we think is best, rather than conforming to what others claim we should do, we have to persist in pursuing our goals, and to continue to act according to our own ideals. Merely succumbing to our relatives' pressures inevitably repeats what was done in the past. However, even though maintaining or increasing our independence may seem to be a relatively insignificant aim, we must be prepared to experience a great deal of stress, tension, and conflict when we go against the flow of interactions in our families, in order to pursue our own goals.

Some of our most tenacious family conflicts remain unresolved for generations. Families with longstanding conflicts frequently have difficulty recalling what the original reasons were for the family estrangements. Even though there are no justifications to carry the conflicts forward to members of the younger generations, these schisms tend to persist. Furthermore, when family members finally make efforts to bridge these estrangements and conflicts, their actions are often resisted by other relatives, including members of those families that have been estranged. Nevertheless, when the family members who want to reconnect with their estranged relatives continue to move in this direction, in spite of their relatives' resistance, the whole family eventually stabilizes and benefits from the re-forged relationships.

The difficulties we have, in acting independently among the complex emotional bonds of several generations of our families, show how challenging pursuing our own goals can be. Similar reactions of family resistance occur when we do whatever our families are not used to, or do not want. Family resistance frequently surfaces in reaction to threatened changes, such as dating across racial or religious lines; coming out of the closet as gays or lesbians; changing careers; or changing jobs. Even though we may understand that this resistance is predictable, we can also learn a great deal from actually feeling the powers of family resistance in our own families. In addition, managing or dealing with our families' resistance increases our social intelligence, and provides us with emotionally strong independence that we can draw upon in varied family and social situations.

When we focus on increasing our independence in our work systems, religious communities, or professional associations, we find that we tend to be rejected or shunned by the group. We need to exercise great caution in these contexts because, unlike our families—who remain connected to us due to their multigenerational or lifetime bonds—these other groups do not have similar emotional investments in our wellbeing or continued membership. Therefore, we will be forcefully expelled by these groups—for example, lose our jobs—if we try to be too independent in these other socially significant settings. Once again we experience directly that successful integration through conformity is how many groups thrive. Truly independent thought and actions often disturb the equilibrium of families and other well-established groups.

The value of being independent in work systems, religious communities, or professional associations pays off in the long run, as long as the innovators prevent group resistance or conflicts from getting out of hand. Innovators who are accepted for their new contributions know how to deal with this predictable opposition, as well as how to create new designs and priorities. Although these processes resemble families' acceptances of innovations, our successes are more precarious in groups than in families. When relationships are not built on the solid foundations of families' emotional systems, the patterns of acceptance in groups are relatively transient and fickle.

Because of the hazards of becoming independent in meaningful social settings, we have to work toward this goal throughout out lives. Increasing our social intelligence as we try to become independent is an effective aid, and increased social intelligence necessarily promotes increased independence throughout all the groups to which we belong. Becoming independent is not a task for the fainthearted, but its rewards—through persistence—are personal, professional, political, and societal.

Families in History

Our families are deeply rooted in local, national, and global histories. Also, when we are socially intelligent, we become historical actors. That is, we act according to our awareness of our social systems' relatedness through time. In addition, we maintain as broad a perspective of history as possible in our actions, so that we are able to connect family events—past and present—with what is going on in society at large.

Families and Social Intelligence

Many of our family histories, and the life outcomes of our relatives, are strongly affected by historical events. For example, wars fought by family members may directly involve deaths or serious injuries, and migrations generally create dramatic political or cultural shifts. The state of economies, as well as past and present political conditions, can be life-threatening, and cause migrations of whole families. Even settlements after migrations can be extremely stressful, affecting family members' decision-making for a lifetime.

Historical conditions influence family well-being through restricted opportunities for well-paid work, ineffective legislation against prejudice and discrimination, and limited or inadequate housing facilities for families. Low pay for the work of young adults, and low educational standards throughout a society, are further examples of historical conditions that restrict the development of human potential. Although these circumstances may change through time, there is often not sufficient political will to bring about improvements in the limiting social conditions, without a great deal of organized agitation against the status quo.

Social intelligence increases when we compile facts about as many generations of our families as possible. This allows us to see patterns of interaction among the different generations—that is, beyond the lifespan of any particular family member—and enables us to be more objective about our families' histories. With this comprehensive historical information in hand, we can identify both functional and dysfunctional patterns of adaptation and behavior in our families. We may more easily understand, for example, what the emotional significance of family conflicts are, and have been, especially those where relatives do not get along with each other for generations.

We also gain social intelligence when we put our family histories into broad social and historical perspectives—by connecting them to local, national, and global trends. This wide-ranging social knowledge enables us to understand more fully why we are who we are. Such a hard-won, vital lesson is often difficult to learn, but it cannot be accomplished by other means.

VIII. How Do We Interact With Families Differently?

Furthermore, it is precisely our particular life-histories, family histories, and local, national, and global histories that make us unique.

When we focus on being historical actors in this holistic way, we become less defined by historical events and social circumstances that are beyond our control. Because we understand ourselves in greater depth and greater breadth, we cease to be easily manipulated. Social intelligence helps us to appreciate the fact that historical influences have considerable power over us, but they do not determine our fates. One of the strongest antidotes we have, for these broad impersonal forces, is to act so that we preserve our objectivity, autonomy, and independence for individual and collective pursuits of social intelligence and social justice.

Becoming more aware of our families in history helps us to realize that our families are history, and that we are necessarily historical actors. This encourages us to use the historical knowledge we gain about our families to act in ways which increase our own and others' social intelligence, as well as preserve and nurture our families. At the same time, we are more able to help launch our young adult relatives into the real, multidimensional world, where much remedial work still needs to be done. Thus, enhancing our capacities to become historical actors also increases social justice.

Although these action strategies may appear to be lofty goals or ideals, being historical actors essentially means that we stay observant and vigilant about our actions. Time becomes a more precious commodity to us, not for the purpose of being paid for our labor, but because our lifetimes and emotional resources are necessarily limited. In order to make the world a better place, we have to plan how we will act in light of our limitations, as well as according to the ideals of social intelligence and social justice.

Being aware of history as social processes makes us more in tune with societies' influences in our lives. For example, we try to identify specific tasks—in our families and in our communities—which need our committed actions, so that we can create better social conditions for all. We also ask ourselves what particular actions we need to consider—for individual, family, and social well-being—as we continue to deepen our understanding of families in society and social justice.

Families in Society

Sometimes it is difficult to believe that what we do in our families affects society. Does what we do in our families really matter when society is so much more complex and vast than our families? How are our actions felt in public spheres, when both common sense and public opinion suggest that our families are "only" private?

Social intelligence narrows the gaps between private and public, and between public and private aspects of our lives. Although our family interactions are not public, in that they are not usually or not easily scrutinized by others, they are public in that they are inextricably tied to societies and the common good. What we do in our families affects our orientations to our relatives, as well as to people outside our families. Furthermore, the given systemness of our families' relationships with the rest of society means that family interactions necessarily infiltrate other groups and social institutions to some extent.

In addition to historical views of our families, the overlap of social systems in societies gives us another dimension of awareness of how deeply rooted our families are in particular societies. In order to think more concretely about the systemness of our families and societies, it is useful to consider how social intelligence emphasizes the power of connections between families and beliefs, families and social classes, families and cultures, and families and history. These connections are deep-seated and primal, and include bonds which remain powerful, because of their emotional and value-laden content. As individuals we choose either to accept this reality of systemness, or to reject it in different degrees. The fact-based foundations of social intelligence derive from a basic acceptance of this connectedness.

VIII. How Do We Interact With Families Differently?

This means that although it is perhaps easier to identify historical links between our families and societies, there are often less obvious or more invisible aspects of social systems' relatedness which are equally powerful. Using social intelligence, especially in order to understand some of the complexities of our relationships to whole societies, is a practical and largely simplified strategy. However, through our own applications of social intelligence, we can prove—at least to ourselves—that social intelligence is also an effective intellectual tool to guide our analyses and actions.

When we consider how to be a good son or a good daughter, for example, we must get beyond our feelings for our parents, so that we can look more closely at how sons and daughters have interacted with their parents and grandparents throughout the different generations of our families, and in our societies. We also need to examine what beliefs we have internalized about sons and daughters from our family cultures and from societies. What are the values we associate with being a good son or a good daughter? What are the dependencies which, as adults, have been continued and repeated in our own specific roles as sons and daughters in our families?

To further this exploration, we also look at our options of how to interact with our parents, grandparents, siblings, and other kin members as sons and daughters. Are there other sons or daughters in our families, for example, who act in ways we would like to emulate? Can we use their examples more deliberately as role models, or should we scrutinize other cultures in order to find ways to interact that are closer to our own beliefs about being responsible sons and daughters?

Considering societies themselves, for more options about how sons and daughters act, includes looking at social class differences in family behavior. Examining varied economic classes, educational levels, genders, sexual orientations, races, ethnicities, and degrees of able-bodiedness gives us broad ranges of possible choices. The contrasting roles of sons and daughters in families help us to gain objectivity about our own responsibilities as sons and daughters, and guide our decisions about which patterns of family interaction to emulate.

It is because of these broad perspectives that social intelligence frequently becomes a significant means of enlightenment. We can teach ourselves, now that we are adults, about options that were not available to us as children. Once we see these alternatives, we can more easily and more effectively design different paths for ourselves as sons and daughters. Social intelligence helps us to address the needs of both our families and our societies, while making deeper commitments to work toward increasing social justice in our troubled world.

IX. How Can We Increase Meaning in Families?

One of the most important benefits of increasing our social intelligence is that the new breadth and depth of these perspectives increases our choices of meanings we can accept or reject. Above all, social intelligence increases our freedom to choose what we do with our lives, and our motivations to act derive largely from the meanings we attribute to our everyday situations.

Finding meaning in what we do on a daily basis is deeply connected to our feelings and emotions, which often have social sources. Our interpretations of facts, and the values we cherish the most, link our emotions to these meanings. However, we can also merely decide to enjoy our lives, even though we may find very few reasons to make our lives meaningful. By contrast, when we make decisions and commitments to add meanings to our lives, we build series of ongoing self-fulfilling prophecies. Meanings exist because we attribute them to what we do, and when we establish choosing our meanings as a high priority, we find them, and consequently change our courses of action.

Social intelligence shows us that we may look for, and find, meanings in order to increase our life-satisfaction for pragmatic reasons. Both finding and creating meanings increase our zest for life, as well as help us to bear the trials and tribulations that necessarily accompany maintaining family relationships or other personal bonds, and conducting our daily affairs.

Furthermore, when we use our social intelligence to see our families differently, and to interact with them differently, our increased objectivity allows us to associate additional historical or social meanings with whatever we do.

Meanings are not static. They change as we learn and act, and we become more adept at deliberately cultivating meanings as we increase our social intelligence. These expanded meanings safeguard our emotional well-being. For example, we do not easily get despondent about our personal relationships, or unmet goals, when we see the broader purposes of what we do. Our deeper attunement to seeking and finding meaning in our actions keeps us motivated, so that we continue to increase our social intelligence, and ultimately act on behalf of social justice.

Being specific about the particular meanings that give us these choices makes significant differences in our lives. In order to achieve this enhancement, we scrutinize the meanings we find through our families, our beliefs, social classes, cultures, and societies. This helps us to see that many of the meanings we harbor may be dysfunctional for us. For example, our meanings may contradict each other, or they may evoke negative feelings about who we are and what we do. Our persistence in using the lens of social intelligence, to examine our meanings, helps us to select which of our social beliefs we need to change, and which will move us forward in our quests to be more enlightened in what we do.

We scrutinize meanings we already use about our families, beliefs, social classes, cultures, and societies before we choose which meanings we really want to keep for our own. We do this because we absorb new meanings more effectively at the same time that we discard the old. Therefore, we need to relinquish those meanings which no longer serve us well in our more socially intelligent ways of being and doing, in order to embrace meanings that motivate us at deeper levels, or which help us to transcend the hassles we inevitably encounter each day.

Because we do not act in a social vacuum, discarding old meanings and accepting new meanings is largely a reciprocal, simultaneous process. We reject our original negative, incompatible meanings, and then necessarily start to absorb new meanings. Furthermore, accepting new meanings increases our motivations to persist in weeding out old meanings which no longer serve us well.

Rejecting and accepting meanings is not a superficial intellectual exercise. Our broader, more socially intelligent thinking and critical reflections are vital, integral parts of absorbing new meanings. By extension, we act as we think, and doing things differently in our families is a tried and tested way to make these new meanings our own. We cannot merely think our way into new orientations. We need to interact with others in order to forge our new meanings, and in order to be able to apply them to whatever we do.

Because new meanings provide new interpretations of individual, family, and social realities, they evoke different values and priorities. Thus our new meanings consistently have powerful impacts on who we are and what we do. As we discard our old meanings, and accept new meanings, we experience the dramatic practical differences that our meanings make to us as we go about our work and play. The effects of clarifying our meanings are tantamount to becoming more inspired and more enlightened, which means that our actions eventually gain a stronger sense of purpose and direction. Our changed meanings generate deep-seated shifts in our behavior, and they are at the core of understanding and applying social intelligence to our families and the rest of our lives.

Choosing Meanings

Social intelligence provides many more options for formulating perspectives and strategies than conventional thinking. When we identify patterns in the overlapping social influences which affect our lives the most, we see both problematic and optimal patterns that we can either change or perpetuate. Thus choosing meanings is an effective strategy for making constructive changes in our life courses and families.

Choosing meanings focuses on, and even calls into question, our usual ways of making decisions. Many of us realize that our childhoods were important, because it is then that we began to accept or reject our parents' values, and later to similarly absorb or discard values of our religions and schools. However, social intelligence helps us to understand that internalizing values is a lifetime process, that is activated in each social situation we face.

It is healthy and empowering to interpret our given or routine social situations differently, as well as to learn new values and skills. Re-aligning our priorities in mid-life, for example, inevitably affects our behavior, and even though these changes may not be welcomed by our families, they have the power to transform our lives and theirs. Re-interpreting, re-learning, and re-defining who we are and how we relate to others increases our social intelligence, enhances our life-satisfaction, and transforms our interactions.

Singling out those values we want to honor through our everyday behavior in our families is an important facet of choosing meanings. We start to reject some of the meanings we do not want to have in our lives—such as ignoring the value of learning—when we first examine more closely how we make decisions, as well as how we interact with our relatives and others. Sometimes it takes particular actions, like identifying educational opportunities for our children, to make us realize the emphases we could give to education in our own lives. For example, taking a positive approach to our children's education may transform our understanding of the power and advantages of learning in our own lives.

When we see the many benefits of learning—for our families, for ourselves, and for society—we often become more effective advocates of both formal education and alternative ways of learning. Changing the meaning of education for ourselves shows us that education is a multi-faceted process, which has a great deal of relevance in all the most complex social situations that confront us. Deep-seated individual and social learning is at the heart of social intelligence, and when we both recognize and value all the learning we do and can do, we strengthen ourselves as well as our contributions to our families and societies.

These changes occur as soon as we begin to modify the meanings we attribute to learning. Learning is no longer a product of authority figures' control over our attention, but rather an exciting option for discovery, which never fails to inspire. Even when we are in difficult or problematic situations, we can find ways to learn whatever we can from our strife and pain. Seeing the broader picture of our suffering consistently helps us to act differently, as well as to re-define our situations more honestly and more creatively.

Choosing new meanings increases our objectivity, and establishes different priorities. We necessarily become less hypocritical in what we do, and social intelligence shows us how to be more aware of the many ways in which we can honor our new values and priorities through our actions. Re-interpreting facts in our families, as well as making different value choices, increases our effectiveness in choosing meanings that we want to develop most in what we do.

Exploring the meanings we find in our families, beliefs, social classes, cultures, and societies shows us that these meanings are sources of our current values and ongoing interpretations of social realities. We also discover that family meanings are frequently the most tenacious and most difficult of our meanings to change.

However, focusing on the sum total of our major beliefs clarifies our understanding of the social sources of our meanings, and makes the task of changing particular meanings more manageable. Looking at meanings in our social classes, cultures, and societies makes us more aware of how our family meanings—such as aversion to learning—are replicated in different social spheres. Seeing and understanding these widespread patterns in our meanings help us to design more effective strategies to change our meanings in our families and other social settings. When our meanings become more coherent, and more consistent, our goal-directed actions are more effective in achieving whatever we value most through our meanings.

Meanings in Families

When we are children, family expectations are often clear-cut and unassailable. For example, we may be asked—or required—to be obedient to elders, and to follow in the footsteps of other family members. Unfortunately these expectations give children limited or unimaginative ideals and meanings, and these same expectations may be held by parents and other relatives indefinitely.

As adults we need to be able to identify the values and meanings that were transmitted to us by our original families, and to find ways—if needed—to change how we behave. It is imperative, as socially intelligent adults, that we question and challenge relatives' definitions of reality, and decide for ourselves which ideals and goals we want to pursue. This posture of questioning and decision-making in our families should be a high priority throughout our lives as adults, as increasing meaning in the context of our families is a significant part of laying foundations for living in more socially intelligent ways.

One of the key ways in which parents transmit meanings to their children is to present ideas and examples of what it is to be a man or a woman. Boys and girls are often trained to accept different moral standards. However, even when we are very young, there may be some disgust and outrage at the double standards in genders that are invoked, accepted, and used by our elders—which is evidence of children's strong senses of fairness or social justice.

Whatever the fads and foibles of a particular family, gender and sex expectations are often thought to be important orientations for members of the youngest generations. As we become adults, even though we may choose to challenge our parents' gender and sexual standards, families continue to try to perpetuate their own beliefs and meanings about gender and sexuality. Some of the tensions in children's and adolescents' responses to parents' gender and sexual expectations result from parents' punitive repercussions for children and adolescents who do not comply. It is often only when we become economically independent that we can identify our own gender roles and sexual orientations autonomously and definitively.

Other very significant values that we absorb as children, such as religion and education, are also filtered through or influenced by parental and family attitudes. Even though most of our exposure and learning in religion and education may ultimately be well beyond the confines of our families, we acquire some of our most essential attitudes to religion and education—such as openness—from our parents or other emotionally significant relatives. Furthermore, even though family elders may stress the importance of religion and education in what they say, it is their actions around religion and education that are remembered and emulated by children, perhaps for a lifetime.

The primary significance of meanings in families, from the point of view of social intelligence, is that meanings are integrated in deep-seated ways, which are consequently difficult to change. The associations and meanings absorbed also represent clusters of values which, when we were young, gave us some degree of security and certainty in a rapidly-changing world. When we are adults, however, these same values and meanings may block our life-satisfaction in important ways. The challenge of social intelligence is to make us question the extent of our acceptance of parental standards, in order to decide which meanings we want to accept or increase for ourselves as adults.

Another aspect of social intelligence is to realize what the overall importance of meanings in our lives implies. For example, in order to be fully human we must accept some values and standards, especially if we want to lead rewarding lives which contribute to others. Human meanings are the basis of civilization, and we cannot reject our family values and meanings without some pain as well as difficulty. Rather, we need to learn how to be more objective and selective about the meanings we accepted as children, so that we can select our most constructive meanings now, in order to orient ourselves to others and the world.

When we scrutinize our family meanings, we predictably find values and meanings we can cherish, as well as those we want to discard. Our choices of which family meanings we want to preserve have powerful consequences, especially as they help us to be both more secure and more authentic in our rapidly changing, complex worlds. Although it is deeply satisfying, for example, to be able to transmit family meanings we received from our parents and grandparents to our children and grandchildren, these meanings must be critically assessed and updated where needed, in order to be consistent with our social intelligence. Thus it is our chosen meanings that have more constructive impacts on our families, social justice, and our worlds.

Meanings in Beliefs

An important fact about our personal beliefs is that they are not only often shared by our families, but they frequently include belief systems. That is, our beliefs are typically not internalized piecemeal as we mature, but rather are clusters of beliefs which are based on a few premises or propositions. For example, even though the individual members of a particular religion have wide variations in the specifics of their actual beliefs and practices, there are also some influential common denominators, or clusters, among these related beliefs.

The meanings in our beliefs derive from both traditional belief systems and fragmented sources. Those belief systems which have the most influence, historically, are often religious or political. A consequence of the power of these belief systems on our well-being is that membership in major world religions, or in major political parties, gives us a sense of identity and belonging, as well as series of related substantive beliefs, values, and meanings.

The sum of our beliefs—both belief systems and fragmented beliefs—yields important meanings as orientations to life, as well as strong motivating forces. Moreover, unless we find real meaning in our lives we become alienated, which prevents us from working toward increasing the common good and social justice. In order to be fully human, and to develop our potentials, we must have appropriate meanings to guide our decision-making, and to direct our actions.

In many respects, social intelligence is a secular belief system. However, even though we are required to test our beliefs in social intelligence, through the facts and experiences of our everyday trial and error applications of social intelligence, many of the assumptions we may make about social intelligence are as yet not formally proved, and rest on our faith in the ideas and ideals of social intelligence. This necessary tentativeness about the complex powers and consequences of social intelligence does not change some of the basic facts of social intelligence. For example, we are more or less socially intelligent, whether we know it or not, and our social intelligence governs much of what we do and how we do it.

Social intelligence is a belief system in part because it is a synthesis of beliefs drawn from our families, religions, social classes, cultures, and politics. These broad and deep social sources of our beliefs need to be examined in relation to our beliefs, because whoever communicated and continues to transmit beliefs to us is emotionally significant in our definitions of individual and social realities. After we locate our beliefs in our families and other social systems, we can be more creative in pulling our chosen beliefs together, so that we have an increasingly coherent belief system to guide us.

An important qualitative dimension of our beliefs and meanings is the degree of open-mindedness or closed-mindedness that accompanies our beliefs. For example, do we cling to what we consider to be absolute truths, which cannot be challenged by facts? Or, are we open to changing and modifying at least some of our beliefs, because of what we learn through our experiences and formal or informal education?

It is also not only what we believe that is socially significant, but how we use our beliefs. For example, are we dogmatic or bigoted in applying our beliefs to everyday life? Do our beliefs serve as rationales for us to be authoritarian in our relations with our families and others? Or, do we stay open, and therefore more objective, in principle, to considering facts, ideas, and beliefs outside our own experiences?

In reviewing our beliefs, and the meanings they provide for our directions and purposes in life, we need to be particularly aware of the power of religious beliefs. One aspect of this power is the systemness of the many different beliefs within each world religion. These religions have persisted through time expressly because they meet complex human needs, especially those which call forth beliefs and rituals to address life's everyday contingencies. Major world religions are powerful because they acknowledge and embrace human frailties, as well as apply to a wide range of diverse social situations. Major world religions, however ancient, also provide institutionalized beliefs and rituals, which cover widely shared experiences of crises and other significant events in families and societies.

Religious denominations, sects, and cults give sacred or supernatural sanctions to particular kinds of behavior. Sharing beliefs in one God in a society, whatever the particular religion, usually automatically evokes a certain degree of respect, attention, and fear, for example. Similarly, the negative sanctions or prohibitions of religions may be as powerful as their rewards for being religious.

Social intelligence guides us to increase our meanings in life by assessing our family beliefs, traditional religions, or secular beliefs. How we interpret traditions and values influences our communications with others—not only because of our beliefs and meanings, but also because of our actions. We are responsible for the beliefs and meanings we cultivate and cherish, especially because it is these beliefs and meanings that essentially govern who we are and what we do. In these ways social intelligence helps us to direct our beliefs, meanings, and actions toward increasing social justice in our families and in society.

Meanings in Social Classes

Whatever the social classes we belong to, each class is supported and maintained by particular meanings. Although changing our own social class meanings does not necessarily change our social class affiliations, it is useful to examine the extent to which our meanings derive from or support our social classes. Demystifying our social class meanings helps us to be more objective about our social class origins, or our social class aspirations, so that we are freer to give our attention and energy to tasks and actions which address the common good more directly.

The basic dimensions of our social classes can be thought of as economic means, educational achievement, gender, sexual orientation, race, ethnicity, and able-bodiedness. Even though the physiological characteristics of some of these social class bases—gender, sexual orientations, race, ethnicity, and able-bodiedness—suggest that we cannot easily change these classes, so that they become more like castes, social intelligence shows us that we can choose more constructive attitudes about our own social classes and social classes in general.

Social intelligence requires that we maintain as much objectivity as possible when we look more closely at our social classes and their meanings, especially with respect to understanding our families. When we become more aware of the history of social classes, for example, we realize that these divisions and schisms have existed since our earliest settled societies, and that it is unlikely that social classes and their meanings will be swept away or transformed in the near future. This suggests, however, that we should take a hard look at our social classes, in order to avoid or neutralize their impositions of false values on our meanings, so that we can move along—in spite of social class restrictions—in a spirit of trying to change social class injustices.

Our mental and emotional imaginings cannot reduce the power of our social classes, but with social intelligence we can choose to shift our attention to those non-class-bound meanings that we want to live by. We lose our freedom when we consistently live according to others' social class standards, for example, because then we orient our limited energies and resources toward goals which do little more than reinforce the status quo, sometimes through our own upward mobility. Having satisfactory standards of living is always important, but these need to be shared more equitably throughout society if the common good is to be increased, and if the ideals and meanings of social justice are to be priorities.

Being more objective about the seemingly bottomless needs for social class maintenance, through our economic resources and educational achievements, makes us aware of the more constructive purposes we could pursue through these same economic and educational resources. Making social justice a priority means that not only will society become a fairer place, but also that many of our most serious social problems—such as poverty and crime—will gradually be controlled and reduced. Thus, when we examine our families' and societies' real needs more closely, rather than merely their consumer wants, we see a different picture of ourselves, our families, and our societies.

In many real respects our families are sources of emotions and meanings for our interactions with those social classes that seem the most significant or most familiar to us. Particular social classes are important orientations in our lives because they were, and are still considered to be so, by our families. This issue of the emotional significance of social classes needs to be explored, before we decide to embrace or discard specific social class meanings. For example, our shared dreams of upward social mobility may need to be put aside, in order to imagine or see how our families and societies would be without the persistently strong influences of social classes.

Whether or not our own families have suffered hardship due to social class privations, our most meaningful decisions may relate directly to improving conditions for those who are unable to help themselves. Assuming meanings which promote advocacy for low status social classes—impoverished groups who lack educational opportunities; women, homosexuals, and bisexuals; less privileged races and ethnic groups; and disabled individuals—can be worthwhile for all individuals, families, and communities. If we are to counteract some of the destructive consequences of social classes, we need to address injustices that restrict opportunities as a high priority. Social intelligence shows us that the quality of life throughout societies depends on refining and balancing the needs of all.

Meanings in Culture

Even though our families often continue to be the primary sources of our meanings throughout our lives, cultural influences from societies inevitably infiltrate family cultures and the meanings held by both adult and child family members. In some instances families develop an "us" against "them" adversarial posture toward external cultural influences: family members close ranks to outsiders to safeguard their own meanings, which may contrast sharply with the broader cultural values held by most people in a society. Families who try to isolate their cultural meanings in this way give a much higher priority to the "us" of family meanings than to the "them" of outsiders, who may call those family meanings into question.

However much families want to isolate themselves from others' meanings, cultural influences are indisputably omnipresent, and pervade all family communications within families and with the outside world. As children grow and mature, they are often enticed by the cultural meanings of outsiders, and sometimes travel overseas in order to satisfy their curiosity. When we live fully, our needs to explore the world drive us forward, and it is ultimately impossible to be satisfied with knowledge that is based only on our families' meanings.

Assessing wide ranges of cultural meanings does not necessitate rebelling against our families' cultural meanings, even though some family members may try to adapt through revolt. It is more realistic, and more mature, to choose to mix and match our cultural meanings, depending on our own experiences and knowledge. Although we need to remain critical of all cultural meanings, social intelligence should guide our critiques and assessments of our families' cultural meanings. For example, we need to be sure that we really do want to substitute others' cultural meanings for some of our families' cultural meanings before we adopt them.

Broad cultural meanings are often based on clusters of values which may seem different from our families' cultural meanings. For example, religious values in traditional societies are frequently more clearly defined than in modern societies, and these religious values frequently maintain a coherence and relevance for everyday life in traditional societies which families' cultural meanings may not provide. Individual members of families in modern societies might be attracted to religions for the meanings they offer, but many religious interpretations of modern everyday realities may also more easily clash with families' views.

Market values tend to dominate family meanings in modern secular societies, so that families and individual members are lured into buying products which enhance their images, or help them to feel as though they play important parts in rapid technological changes. Purchasing products may distance some consumers from their families, but this difference in meanings is often resolved by families' gradual acceptances of more materialistic cultural meanings.

Because education broadens our horizons, and social intelligence helps us to see ourselves and our worlds differently, we necessarily transcend some of our original family meanings as we mature. Due to the wide variety of cultural meanings available to us in modern societies, it is useful to choose cultural meanings which give us a sense of purpose and direction. We need to ask ourselves what it is that we want to learn or do in society, which can be expedited through embracing particular cultural meanings. Or, how can we most meaningfully learn about positions that we want to hold, or tasks that we really want to accomplish?

IX. How Can We Increase Meaning in Families?

Social intelligence helps us both to preserve our loyalties to our families' meanings—to the extent that they continue to inspire us—and to select new cultural meanings. Although cultural meanings often ultimately motivate us to make innovations in our families and societies, they first show us how to redefine ourselves, our families, and our societies.

Some cultural meanings may motivate us to make policy or legal changes. At the same time that broad cultural meanings change, widespread changes in behavior in societies occur. Also, if we pursue ideals of social justice, we may assume cultural meanings that are different from those of our families, in order to make innovations that increase the common good. Our deliberately selected families' meanings and cultural meanings produce the quality of inspiration that will sustain us when our progress is difficult. We need ongoing quests to discover which cultural meanings and values we can deliberately cultivate and cherish, so that they will carry us forward through the adversities that will inevitably occur in our families and in our societies.

Meanings in Society

If we were raised in families which value political parties and political participation, we are likely to have developed a fairly astute awareness of society as a whole, societies, and the difference that ideas make to family and social well-being. However, because all too often rather narrow self-interests are represented by particular political policies, it is again necessary to use the broad perspectives of social intelligence to sort out which meanings about families and societies we want to make our own.

Meanings in society, and meanings about society, go beyond political definitions. They include the sense we make of history, evolution, and globalization, as well as ways to understand the complexities of different societies. These major social influences are impossible for human beings to grasp objectively or fully, but in order to survive we need to have some viable working ideas of their significance in our lives, and in the lives of others. For example, it is difficult to imagine what more constructive futures for our families and societies would look like, unless we make some assumptions about history, evolution, and globalization.

Social intelligence helps us to be more aware of the assumptions we make about societies. The breadth of perspectives of social intelligence enables us to think differently from more conventional approaches to interpreting social realities. Above all, social intelligence builds knowledge on the key assumptions that human beings are social at their core, and that they cannot make societies more just without realizing the impact of social influences on their individual and collective freedoms. From this socially intelligent perspective, short term political policies are predictably doomed to fail in attaining social justice, unless they are based on a deep understanding of the social needs and social characteristics of their societies.

The view that societies form a world system, which is made up of overlapping social systems, is a central aspect of social intelligence. Because of its breadth and complexity, this view allows us to make varied interpretations of values and meanings. However, we can also more easily see that one of the essential characteristics of individuals, families, and societies is that they are interdependent, and that much interaction and meaning is explained by this interdependency.

Even though we need each other in order to survive, our experiences of interacting with our families show that interpersonal and group dynamics must honor both unity and individuality or uniqueness, if we are to find fulfillment and achieve our goals. This means that if we work only toward constructing families or societies with high degrees of harmonious interdependence, we may be pleasing others rather than working toward our own goals, with the result that we are likely to become apathetic and lose some of our inventive talents. Thus, in considering what an optimal society would be like, we understand that we must work with both social tensions—toward unity and toward individuality—so that we can effectively increase the common good in the long run.

IX. How Can We Increase Meaning in Families?

One of the meanings we discern from these applications of social intelligence is that society is not the enemy that must be changed, or overthrown by anarchic individual choices. Rather, society originally and ultimately saves us. However, this is not the whole story: we have a moral imperative to improve social conditions, so that all can benefit from our social riches sooner rather than later. We are here not only to meet our individual and family needs, but also to assess the needs of individuals, groups, communities, and societies beyond our families. Thus we must contribute to the world, as well as meet our family responsibilities for those who depend on us, if we are to be fulfilled.

When we deliberately orient ourselves to these tasks, examining societies' meanings motivates us to locate resources, opportunities, and skills. For example, we decide how to learn more about societies, so that we have richer resources to use. If we understand the particular meanings that jobs, professions, social movements, or political parties hold for us, we make more socially intelligent choices about our being and doing in the world. Also, if we cannot find what we really want in societies, we can make whatever commitments are necessary for creating the resources and opportunities we need.

The challenge to use social intelligence to choose our own meanings makes us consider meanings in our families, beliefs, social classes, cultures, and societies. We cannot find meanings in a vacuum, and we cannot understand meanings in our societies without considering links among meanings in our families, beliefs, social classes, cultures, and societies.

When we are socially intelligent, we are aware of these complex social systems, and think in terms of social systems rather than individually, or according to social conventions. Individualistic dimensions of social realities are too limited to change the world, and conventional thinking is so much a product of particular societies that it cannot consistently inspire appropriate solutions for our toughest, most complex global issues. However, because social intelligence links the different perspectives of families, beliefs, social classes, and cultures to societies, it helps us to create new ways of thinking and doing, especially for designing new means to increase social justice

.

Families and Social Intelligence

X. How Families Threaten Social Intelligence

Social intelligence is not a friend to most families, at least not initially. In the short run, social intelligence inevitably destabilizes families' emotional systems. This is so because social intelligence requires individual family members to be more autonomous, and eventually to act toward establishing freedom for all. The more thoughtful behavior of family members who practice social intelligence necessarily challenges family togetherness, which is often mistakenly believed by most family members to be family harmony. The increased independence of the more socially intelligent family members upsets some of the traditions and cultures that their families have formed and sustained over the years.

In principle, social intelligence challenges families to examine themselves, and then change how they interact. However, because family members who initiate socially intelligent moves seem to be out of line with their relatives, these remaining family members predictably gradually close ranks to form a united front to block those who practice social intelligence. When these pressures, both overt and covert, are brought to bear on the socially intelligent family members, they are strongly encouraged to go back to their former behavior. Their families' resistance to social intelligence essentially threatens their continued development of social intelligence. Consequently, those family members who chose to act according to social intelligence are faced with a quandary.

Should they continue to act according to social intelligence principles, or should they conform to the needs and expectations of their relatives?

Families' resistance to social intelligence can be intense, and may even include dramatic emotional reactions that threaten each person, who is trying to act according to social intelligence, with varied rejections or family expulsion. However, because family bonds—either positive or negative—usually have considerable strength and tenacity, relatives' actions are unlikely to culminate in coercing the more socially intelligent family members to leave their families. Furthermore, families' emotional threats usually decrease through time, especially when those practicing social intelligence stay in meaningful contact with significant family members, while at the same time continuing to develop and increase their social intelligence.

Families do not always lodge such conspicuous threats against family members who choose to be socially intelligent. Also, social intelligence guides us to become more aware of how family threats are expressed, so that we more effectively defuse the tense and difficult situations that predictably arise. Dysfunctions of family members are examples of less direct ways in which families often unintentionally protest social intelligence. When relatives are not aware of the degree and extent of their own resistance to other family members' increased social intelligence, illness or addictive behavior may surface as reactions to family members' socially intelligent moves.

Families that routinely resist new ways of socially intelligent thinking and doing, through forming informal alliances among family members, create particularly weighty threats to the development of a relative's social intelligence. These powerful stands are threatening because such alliances often involve family members from several generations. Families increase their emotional power when they stay connected to members of the older generations, who frequently have additional resources like authority, tradition, and material assets.

X. How Families Threaten Social Intelligence

Perhaps the most significant dimension of families' experiences of turmoil, when a family member acts with social intelligence, is the nuclear family of the socially intelligent family member. Nuclear families easily become overloaded with additional stresses. In this situation, where one nuclear family member becomes more socially intelligent, the nuclear family may cut itself off—or fragment—from the rest of the kin group. Such separations of nuclear families and their extended kin groups weaken the families concerned.

Instead of forming alliances to directly pressure a socially intelligent family member to go back to former patterns of behavior, some members of the socially intelligent person's nuclear family may dysfunction. This more passive threat is predictably reduced in the long run, however, if the socially intelligent family member persists in acting in the same direction, and at the same time relates meaningfully to members of the nuclear family. Gradually, the other nuclear family members usually find more constructive ways to adapt to their family member's increased social intelligence.

Family threats against social intelligence may also be resolved by acquiring sufficient social and emotional skills to deal with relatives' reactions. Focusing on self more effectively, for example, increases the confidence of the socially intelligent family members who decide to come out of the closet about being socially intelligent, specifically about their seeing and doing things differently. A high degree of awareness and alertness is necessary to achieve this kind of resolution, because being socially intelligent is often resisted or protested in hidden ways—especially when family traditions and family dreams are questioned or criticized, as well as when family futures are faced differently. The predictable resistance of family members continues to threaten individuals' progress in developing their social intelligence, until most family members accept at least some of the new orientations of social intelligence.

Intergenerational Currents

As we get to know the systemness of our families better, we become aware of the importance of vertical connections among relatives and their generations: for example, children, parents, grandparents, great grandparents, and beyond. All too often modern thinking about families emphasizes the horizontal dynamics of families, especially between siblings and couples. Although horizontal relationships are also significant in family emotional systems, they are not all-important, nor are they usually as powerful, or as deep-seated, as vertical relationships.

Social intelligence introduces a corrective to these distortions by aiming for increased objectivity. In order to fully understand how our families operate, it is crucial to concentrate on the qualities of vertical relationships in families, as well as their horizontal bonds. Furthermore, it is more socially intelligent to see that what goes on between parents and children in the youngest generations is strongly influenced by how this parent generation was raised by their parents—the children's grandparents. The reciprocity of influences between parents and children is an unbroken intergenerational chain, whether or not we have sufficient information to understand the significance of these important patterns.

Patterns in couples' behavior also depend in part on vertical intergenerational influences. Two-person relationships, in the most recent generations of families, repeat some of the patterns in each partner's parental relationships in the prior generation, as well as backwards through past generations. In these ways we are who we are because of the emotional family systems we belong to, not only in the present moment, but also throughout our families' histories. Because these family roots are deep and powerful, the quality of family links and connections to past generations must be considered—as carefully as possible—when assessing present family problems through applying principles of social intelligence.

This socially intelligent view, of the complex relationships and influences in families, shows us what the emotional power of families is like, and how it may determine the life-courses of the most vulnerable family members. Family pressures—especially when they represent more than one individual's behavior—activate emotional currents of the past, even though the details and dimensions of these influences may be difficult to identify or understand. Given this intrinsic lack of clarity, social intelligence is a useful tool to unravel some of these complexities, so that we can decipher more of our vital family patterns, as well as their implications for us and for others.

Families often summon some of their multigenerational emotional powers when needed. If one family member attempts to do things differently—whether or not this new behavior is inspired by social intelligence—the most dominant family members predictably reactivate latent family alliances, so that these effective pressures can be exerted on the individuals concerned. This dynamic is first seen when parents unite to discipline their young or adolescent children. Parental alliances under stress frequently expand to include other relatives, the most powerful alliances being vertical kin relationships, which then work together with the horizontal bond of parents in the nuclear family.

When adult children introduce prospective mates or partners to their parents, strong negative reactions from the parents are predictable if they do not like, or do not approve of, these individuals. Even though the parents' adult children may have routinely made responsible choices and commitments in the past, these facts may be discounted during the present parental opposition. Furthermore, the family pressures of parental and intergenerational alliances may become sufficiently powerful to dissuade the young family members from pursuing their relationships, or they may draw the new couples closer together through their negative reactions to parents' and other kin members' opposition to their partners.

Whatever the outcomes of these family tensions, intergenerational alliances are consistently powerful. In extreme cases, adult children who do not back out of parentally disapproved relationships may be completely shunned by their kin. The parents of these adult children may treat them as deceased, for example, with other relatives following suit. The immature behavior of these elders creates severe family problems for their whole families, as well as for the responsible adult children.

So how can social intelligence be an effective and meaningful guide in these family crises? Adult children who continue to have meaningful contact with their families, whatever the specific crisis conditions, will increase their social intelligence, even if they decide to formalize their ties with their new partners or spouses. Although there may be no apparent constructive consequences of the adult children's efforts to maintain family contacts in the short run, in the long run they will be more appreciated, at least indirectly, and their families will have more mature and more balanced relationships.

Some of the reconnections made by the young adults with their conflicted families do not necessarily take place as gradual processes through time, but rather sporadically, especially during family emergencies. When a shunned adult child responds meaningfully and actively to family crises such as deaths of relatives, for example, these upheavals in family relationships make it easier to build more mature family bonds based on social intelligence.

Parents and Children for Ever?

From an evolutionary perspective, some of our commonly accepted beliefs about families—that the primary purposes of families are giving our children legitimacy, protection, and sustenance—are relatively recent. In the last century, public opinion and our legal systems placed more emphasis on how to rear children, and on the growing diversity of our family structures. These conventional views of families are reflected in our "common sense," which often contrasts with social intelligence. For example, social intelligence is distinctive in highlighting important nuances and complexities of family emotional systems, and in using broader perspectives of social influences, as well as more objectivity, to understand families than conventional thinking does.

X. How Families Threaten Social Intelligence

Many contemporary child-focused societies align children's interests with family well-being, which reinforces connections between considering family responsibilities together with children's needs. Nurturing children is certainly a basic human task, which families often perform well. Furthermore, because of the many physical and emotional dependencies of children, this core activity has considerable pragmatic value for human survival. However, when families are seen only as existing for the sake of children, some important realities are distorted. In fact, families meet many varied human needs, being the only social institution to do so. Consequently, social intelligence suggests that civilization, as well as the survival of the human race, depends especially on the overall strength and versatility of our families, which also meet child care needs.

We become more human, and more social, through our families, and we are more likely to reach our human potential because of the wide range of interactions with our families that necessarily go beyond child care necessities. Recent developments in nuclear families, during the last century, resulted in large part from the increased geographical mobility that began in early stages of the industrial revolution. The nuclear families that resulted from the geographical mobility of some pioneering family members tended to become increasingly child-focused, because they were made up only of parents and their children. These new nuclear families often became isolated from their original kin groups, denied the importance of their kin members, and distorted the complexities and balances of their families' emotional systems.

Cultural emphases on the importance of nuclear families also contradict social intelligence. Powerful, widely-held beliefs about nuclear families' significance as the dominant, most adaptive type of modern families, for example, are often based on false assumptions, which most people think should not be challenged. By contrast social intelligence maintains that human needs necessarily go beyond the particular strengths and capabilities of nuclear families, and that our shared needs for emotional security can only be met by staying in meaningful contact with our complex kin groups.

Social intelligence suggests that one reason for the high divorce rates in modern societies is that nuclear families have become overburdened by child care responsibilities. Nuclear families' emphases on meeting children's needs, as well as their fragmentation from kin groups, make it difficult for parents or spouses to develop sufficient support for their own needs. The two-person relationships in marriages, partnerships, or nuclear families are often too fragile and too precarious to meet most coupling or parenting needs, unless they are at the same time connected with their kin groups.

Social intelligence requires us to get outside conventional ways of looking at families as being made up only of parents and children, in order to see intergenerational connections and kin group dynamics for what they are, and what they could be. We need to understand, for example, that our families are complex multigenerational emotional systems, which are basic means of survival, rather than merely passive adaptations to historical shifts or economic pressures. Social intelligence shows us how to find shared historical and cultural characteristics among our diverse families, especially when we think of our families as some of the most meaningful and significant ways to connect us to our past, present, and future societies.

Although parents and children are common denominators of some families, that are sometimes optimal ways to rear children, this emphasis falls short of grasping the complexity of family emotional systems that meet a broader range of general human needs. Social intelligence draws our attention to the fact that although parents and children serve as foundations for many current families, families are much more complex and nuanced than this. The families we need for our present-day survival, and for the continued development of our civilizations, must more realistically depend on active and meaningful participation in complex multigenerational relationships and processes.

X. How Families Threaten Social Intelligence

Social intelligence deepens our understanding of families as complex relationship systems. This does not necessarily mean that new kinds of families need to be developed, but rather that we should use social intelligence to understand the complex realities of families that already exist. Even the simplest nuclear families have complex multigenerational emotional relationship systems that need to be seen, acknowledged, and understood, rather than denied. By holding on to our fixed conventional views about the value of nuclear families, we decrease our capacities to see and cherish the subtle, but sometimes lethal, complexities of family kin relationships, which can make or break our futures. Families must be more than efficient means to raise our children, and social intelligence can lead us to deeper understandings of what families are really all about.

Out of the Closet

Because of the many ways in which families threaten social intelligence, it is important to think through how we are going to approach applying social intelligence principles in our families. In the early stages of using social intelligence to guide our family decisions, we experiment with social intelligence by deliberately doing things differently. At this point there is no reason to justify to our relatives what we are doing, because most of the time we conduct ourselves in fairly familiar ways. In these respects we develop personal, in-the-closet, modified ways of interacting with our relatives.

As time goes by, however, we become more adept at applying social intelligence principles in our exchanges with our families, and our actions may evoke some reactions and resistance from our relatives. However, rather than make declarations about what our socially intelligent intentions are, it is usually wiser to go with the flow of casual communications, at the same time keeping on track with our continued efforts to be more socially intelligent. If our relatives ask us to explain ourselves, it is generally more effective to give some fairly plausible reasons for why we decided to act in certain ways, rather than to describe directly how we see and do things differently because of our new understanding and appreciations of social intelligence.

The main reason for taking such a cautious approach, especially in relation to our families, is that our emotional involvement with these significant others makes us sensitive and reactive to their views of what we do, as well as to what they would think and say about social intelligence. Even though we may not feel very connected to our kin, being members of the same family emotional system for a lifetime means that we have a more intensely interdependent relationship with our relatives, than with members of other groups.

Deliberately being in the closet about our socially intelligent intentions, during the first year or so of trying to apply these principles in our families, protects us from intense negative family reactions. It also gives us more time and breathing space to assess our own motives, as well as to understand social intelligence more fully, especially at the level of taking action. We do not need to evoke family criticism and resistance to what we do and say unnecessarily, especially when we can opt to delay such reactions until we are sufficiently ready and skilled to deal with them.

The threat that exists, when we apply social intelligence in our families, works in two ways: social intelligence threatens the status quo of our families; and families threaten the progress we make in applying social intelligence to our families. When we learn how to be more objective, and what it is we really want to do differently in our families, we are in better positions to handle both threats and challenges. We take care of ourselves and our families more effectively when we are more practiced in applying social intelligence, and we also become more responsible in interacting with others when we increase our social intelligence.

We are not obligated to explain to our families, at any point along the way, that we are applying social intelligence principles. However, in due course, a practical way to come out of the closet to our relatives is to be as open as possible about our reasons for our actions, perhaps mentioning that we are learning about social intelligence. Even though we may hope that social intelligence will change the ways in which our relatives interact in our families, it is more likely to have this effect if we do not make claims about social intelligence, but rather just live according to its principles.

When we act according to social intelligence, we may be asked about what our thinking is. This is an opportunity to open up more about social intelligence, or about decisions we made and why we made them. When there is genuine interest, need, or motivation on the part of our relatives, we can be more open with them about our understanding of social intelligence, and about the differences it has made in our lives.

These strategies of coming out of the closet gradually, with respect to social intelligence, or of not coming out of the closet at all, control negative family reactivity and prevent any inclinations we might have to try to "convert" our relatives to social intelligence. One of the strengths of social intelligence is that applying its principles makes a difference in achieving our most desired goals, and in increasing meaningful satisfaction. These tangible rewards may motivate relatives and others to learn about and live according to social intelligence. Furthermore, we do not have to try to change our relatives directly because our interactions with them are different now, due to our increased social intelligence, and we know that their reactions to us will usually be more accommodating in the long run.

Because of this reciprocity in our emotional needs, we may choose to come out of the closet sufficiently to show our relatives a few principles of social intelligence indirectly, through applying social intelligence to our own everyday lives. However, in most instances it is easier to teach social intelligence to the children in our families, because they are usually eager to learn, and do not resist new ways of looking at the world.

Family Traditions

Traditions are powerful because they can be used as sources of authority in many diverse situations. As we become adults we understand more fully the power of social forms and practices that endure the passage of time beyond a life-span. We begin to see that traditions represent not only particular patterns of behavior, which have been established for at least a few decades, but also patterns that are rooted in past centuries.

Social intelligence requires us to be respectful of traditions, because these often represent the values and ideals of a majority of families, work-places, communities, or societies, as well as define how particular actions are taken. For example, traditions are blueprints for appropriateness, respectability, and gaining social acceptance. As authorities, however, traditions can easily overwhelm the initiatives of individuals, and thereby threaten progress in the already difficult task to increase social intelligence.

Traditions are very much part of young children's lives, even though most children are neither fully aware of these patterns of behavior, nor able to distinguish traditions from the authority of their parents. Traditions permeate everything we do to some extent, because they exist in all social settings. Traditions are the cores of our cultures, and they are sustained by long-established values and meanings.

It is because of these characteristics that traditions, particularly family traditions, may threaten or challenge our new-found social intelligence, especially when we try to do things differently in our families. For example, when we get out of step with what is usually done in our families, or suggest new approaches to organizing family get-togethers which have been established for several generations, our relatives may quickly quash our efforts. Furthermore, even though we understand intellectually that our families will resist our innovations, when family traditions are evoked and supported by our kin, we often feel as though our very being is threatened.

Traditions mark significant events in families, and are frequently associated with rites of passage. Even before children are born, families are prepared for the major event of a birth by traditions that are usually followed by expectant parents. Similarly the birth of a child is often accompanied by particular religious rituals, which reinforce traditions of life-course expectations for children and adults within different families. Courtship, engagement, marriage, and death rituals also have their own specific family traditions, which mark the passage of time in the life-spans of individuals and their families, and increase the social and emotional significance of these milestone events.

One of the most efficient and most effective aspects of traditions is that they enable us to face many contingencies, dealing with them in practical and socially acceptable ways. Our families become more integrated through traditions, for example, and they make effective adaptations to societies through traditions. As children we may have felt, and can still recall as adults, the overwhelming power of traditions, which made us revere traditions and call upon them for guidance. In these respects traditions usually support conformity, because they enable us to follow more closely in the footsteps of our ancestors.

However, life is not merely about conforming to long-established precedents. Social intelligence urges us to respect and learn from traditions, but also to concentrate on designing new and more effective ways of doing things, so that we can solve some of the serious social problems we have, and move more directly toward social justice. At the same time we need to be cautious, because however brave our spirits of innovation are, they are also frail. It is easy to feel threatened, or even annihilated, by traditions. After we use social intelligence to sort out what we want to do differently in our families, running into the resistance and force of family traditions can make us give up our efforts to increase our social intelligence. This means that before we are able to make a good start in applying our socially intelligent plans and intentions, traditions may persuade us to abandon them.

Because respect for traditions is often a deep-seated part of ourselves, we may not only choose to draw upon traditions as sources of knowledge in family crises, but also to see them as ever-present realities in our daily thinking and doing. Traditions are accessible to us at all times and in all places, regardless of whether we choose to consider tradition as a personal guide or not.

If we are not aware of the extent to which tradition dominates our lives, and do not deliberately think for ourselves, tradition can take over what we do. For example, if we are preoccupied with worldly success and upward social mobility, we may continue to strive for social class acceptance and success in particular work systems throughout our lives, without any deep reflection or questioning about the purposes of our lives. This more or less automatic behavior of following traditions and rituals ultimately makes us less alive, and reduces our potentials. Even though such a drastic price may be paid when we succumb to traditions, we may never realize that we are doing this.

By contrast, however disconcerting it may be to ask questions about ourselves, our families, our communities, and our societies, the trajectory of becoming increasingly socially intelligent has the great advantage of keeping us on our toes, as well as open to opportunities to make the world a better place in the present and the future. This is a more valuable option than lulling ourselves into following the dictates of family and social traditions year after year, which may ultimately threaten the social intelligence of the next generations of our children as well as our own.

Family Dreams

Our dreams in the present build our futures, or at least pathways toward those futures. Dreams are produced by the meanings we hold most dear, and from the hopes we cherish for better lives. The substance of our dreams is derived from our cultures, and our dreams express our most meaningful symbols and values.

If we do not dream, we tend to course along with our daily activities haphazardly. Usually, our human fondness for habit and routine saves us from too much disorder in how we conduct ourselves. However, a dreamless life is one that is not entirely our own. In taking things as they come, with no particular ideals and goals to pursue, we risk falling into the trap of leading a life of comfortable conformity, rather than living in order to make creative and innovative contributions.

Groups such as our families, communities, or societies consist of collective dreams as well as individuals. Our collective dreams often express political or social ideals, especially in times of international strife. Dreams are, in part, a resolution of inner tensions: we visualize how things can be better in our dreams, and sometimes this may include life after death.

Dreams are not incidental or unimportant. They have powerful influences over our behavior, especially in respect of how we orient ourselves to act and face the future. The danger of dreams, and how they threaten our social intelligence, is that they are often built on premises of desire, longing, or yearning that may not have any clear bearing on our present situations. We cannot usually dream ourselves out of our problems until we understand what our problems are, for example. However, some dreams may be constructive in spite of the strength of our questionable underlying desires. They can motivate us to take actions to reduce poverty, or other harsh living conditions, without knowing all the facts of these realities.

Above all we need to know whether the dreams we dream are our own dreams, and whether they are in our own interests. Family dreams can be based on securing better futures for all family members, at the same time focusing sharply on how this is to be achieved. However, if our family dreams are too specific about how our happiness is to be achieved, they may not meet particular individual needs, or help to develop individual talents. Ideally socially intelligent dreams are based on family members' potentials, so that they include choices that different family members make to pursue their own goals.

Family dreams that threaten social intelligence are those that try to make family members over in the image of the most dominant family members. In fact, one powerful family member may articulate a dream that essentially establishes a foundation for building a dynasty according to that person's ideals and preferences. Such a powerful dream would influence choices about the best possible education for children and grandchildren, while preparing them to work in the family business.

Lives may be essentially pre-formed by family dreams. This trajectory is often thought of as a privilege, especially by outsiders to these families, but there have also been many unhappy results from the repercussions of dominant family members' dreams. Such dreams can stultify the creativity and social intelligence of the so-called beneficiaries, for example, so that individual family members feel suffocated, largely because they cannot dream for themselves, or even think clearly and independently. Others' dreams for us easily become real threats to our social intelligence, because we are vulnerable to losing ourselves in family dreams that are not our own. Even though it may appear that we have chosen to go in a particular family-determined direction, it is often more accurate to say that we have been conditioned to accept this as our destiny, rather than allowed or encouraged to carve out our own dreams and our own futures.

Social intelligence helps us to discover what our family dreams are, and how we have been affected by them. We need to recall—or ask other family members about—some of the ways we have been described by our relatives from childhood, particularly by our parents. As we became aware that we needed to establish independent directions for ourselves, were we encouraged to do so? Was finding our way a give-and-take process, where we articulated our own dreams? Or, were we encouraged to live out other family members' ready-made dreams?

It is important to use social intelligence to assess the dreams we harbor, and to form the most constructive dreams we can of what we want to contribute to others, as well as of how we want to be in relation to them. We use our social intelligence to minimize threats to our social intelligence, by examining the authenticity of our dreams very closely. If we are to live fully now and in the future, we need to dream our own dreams today. Dreams are powerful individual and social tools, which open doors for us, and fuel our socially intelligent fact-finding approaches to testing reality and changing it.

Family Futures

If families continue to interact in present generations as they did in the past, and do not seek to bring about change for the better in their emotional relationship systems, their futures will greatly resemble their pasts. However, if families open up their emotional relationship systems, through interrupting dysfunctional customary patterns of behavior that have been established for generations, they will have different relationships in the future.

Of all social groups, families are particularly resistant to change, as well as especially persistent in their tendencies and inclinations to reinforce their already-established patterns of interaction. Families resist change in part because of the emotional intensities that flow from their lifetime memberships and multigenerational connections. We have lifetime contractual family relationships—such as marriage and adoption—as well as lifetime family relationships based on blood ties. Because of these facts, repeated patterns of reciprocal behavior are seen more clearly in families than in other social groups. These repetitions are characteristics of the emotional systems of multigenerational interactions during family members' lifetimes.

A family rationale, which is widely used, is that patterns of interaction among our ancestors, as well as among recently deceased family members, must be beneficial for the present and future because they endured until now. This way of looking at the past to justify the present and future is closed-ended, however, in that it implies that we should reproduce the past in our family futures.

Another powerful influence in maintaining the family status quo through the generations to the future is the emotional intensity of the bonds between living and deceased relatives.

For example, we may be more likely to follow in the footsteps of members of past generations in our families when we feel a deep sense of kinship with them, because the emotional systemness of our families predisposes us to repeat continuities from the past to the future. Family futures therefore often seem to be somewhat predetermined, because they are strongly reinforced by our emotional dependencies.

Social intelligence is a particularly effective kind of intervention in these more or less predictable patterns of family processes. If any one family member can interrupt patterns of interactions among past and present family members, the entire family may change in the future. When family interventions open up families' relationship systems, including their links to the past, future patterns of behavior are more distinctly different from the past and present.

An important challenge of social intelligence, in the long run, is to make deliberate interventions in our families. Families which become more open to questioning their pasts, rather than merely repeating them, are more able to orient their younger members to live effectively in improved family futures. Important family knowledge is transmitted through learning or teaching social intelligence to current and future generations, so that increased social intelligence can continue to transform well-being and productivity in these families.

The taken-for-granted orientation of many families toward their futures threatens this optimal application of social intelligence. This is so because the thing that many families seem to want to do most, at their deepest levels of emotional dependency, is to maintain the status quo. This goal makes initiatives and innovations particularly difficult for families to accomplish. Furthermore, family resistance to social intelligence creates strong bulwarks of relatives, who unify emotionally, to ensure that innovations or social intelligence do not disrupt their families.

One way for social intelligence to survive this kind of family resistance is to connect with social influences outside the families. Changing how relatives are educated, or work, for example, creates internal shifts in families, which loosen up what seemed to be unyielding family alliances. Using new ways to express grief when family members die, is another effective approach to accomplish the gradual, difficult, and complex task of opening up families' emotional systems for more beneficial futures.

A strong motivating factor, which helps us to persist in applying principles of social intelligence in our families, is to remember that without our interventions the fates of particular families may be somewhat doomed. Although we may know ways to strengthen our families, the effort is too much, or the conditions too daunting. However, reminding ourselves that without our socially intelligent initiatives, the children yet to be born in our families will have more limited futures, we can work harder toward opening up our families for constructive changes.

XI. Reverence for the Power and Complexity of Families

E ven though it is usually easier to recognize patterns of interaction in our families than in other social groups, understanding families is incredibly challenging. Our families constantly confront us with many enduring mysteries and bafflements, and it is predictably very difficult—often impossible—to have any degree of meaningful control over those we love. Although social intelligence gives us some dependable principles with which to approach the power and complexity of our families, this knowledge is necessarily limited.

We often express the hope that we will build more reliable knowledge about our families in the future. However, it seems that there will always be a great deal of family information and family know-how that we cannot completely grasp with our human minds. In the meantime, it is practical to deliberately sustain a deep awareness of and appreciation for the power and complexity of our families. This approach prevents us from trying to play God with ourselves or our relatives, and encourages us to move forward and onward, in face of the power and complexity of our families, when we experience problematic dependencies and aggravating family issues.

Families are important foundations of our social intelligence, because much of our survival and day-to-day behavior derives from these deep-seated emotional bonds that orient us to self and society. Some of the social survival and fulfillment perspectives we learn from our families, as we grow to maturity, define crucial aspects of our existence: time, space, roles, responsibilities, life, and death. These perspectives influence our individual and social attitudes, as well as our behavior, and have strong impacts on the quality of our lives and their outcomes.

The importance of family definitions of time goes beyond family histories, although understanding major family events and family players through time is an important aspect of how particular families deal with time through the generations. We need to understand the impact of broad historical influences on our family histories and on ourselves. In addition, families have cultures which emphasize the past, the present, or the future. Social intelligence helps us to discern the effects of these differently patterned expressions of the passage of time, as well as to bring them into better balance with each other where necessary.

Space, another dimension of families' complexities, can be understood in part through mapping out geographical moves our family members have made. Local, national, and international migrations cause variations in family behavior which were, and continue to be, strongly influenced by geographical distance and regional or international differences. Social intelligence helps us to be aware of how a few or many contacts with geographically distant relatives can change patterns of family interaction throughout the generations.

Some of the basic roles we play within our families are reinforced—or challenged—by societal norms. For example, the roles of child, sibling, adolescent, adult, parent, or grandparent are central in family interactions and in societies. However, because life is dynamic, our roles are not fixed, and we make many role changes as we grow older. Furthermore, our family role definitions are usually inadequate, and social intelligence suggests that we need to do much more than respond to others' role expectations. Social intelligence shows us the extent to which our families encourage us to conform or deviate from their role definitions, and how we should put our own views of who we are, as individuals, ahead of our relatives' role expectations.

Because families are emotionally interdependent relationship systems, we derive benefits from sharing responsibilities for family members' survival and well-being. Optimally, as very young children, we learn how to be responsible, and although the tasks for which we are responsible change dramatically as we mature, we often strive to act responsibly throughout our lives, so that we and our families do well. Social intelligence guides us in the important tasks of selecting our responsibilities, and helps us to implement them in appropriate ways. Assuming more than an adequate share of responsibilities in our own families may be problematic, for example, because this curtails our capacities to take on broader social responsibilities.

Families orient us toward life, and ideally provide us with emotional security, so that we can live productively and meaningfully. Our understanding of what life is originates in our families. If this basic working knowledge is distorted, we need to change it, because it influences a great deal of what we do on a daily basis, when we are adults as well as when we are children. Social intelligence encourages us to be more objective and more critical about the orientations we received—and still receive—from our families, so that we can construct more reliable and more satisfying ways to understand life.

Families also give us our first experiences of death and losing loved ones. We learn a great deal about our families from how they handle crises and losses. Family upheavals help us to understand who our relatives really are, and how much our intergenerational relationships influence what we see and what we do—not only in our families, but in society. Although patterns of illness and causes of death are significant parts of our family histories, dwelling on genetic links in family illnesses and deaths may not be as productive as using social intelligence to decipher some of the powerful and complex exchanges in our families that occur around illnesses and deaths, which we may be able to change.

Time

Among the many mysteries related to the power and complexity of the influence of time in families are facts about our births and deaths. For example, sometimes our births and deaths have parallels in our family histories: we may have been born on the same day of the year as another relative—living or deceased—or we were born on the same day of the year that a relative died. Although such coincidences may be exaggerated by superstition in some family cultures, it is interesting to reflect on the fact that the timing of family births, marriages, and deaths does not always seem to be entirely random.

Because family histories are inextricably tied to broad societal histories, national events like wars have very strong impacts on family processes. The number of children born in families during wartime is greatly reduced, for example, in part due to the absence of one or both parents who are in the armed services, or because of the high level of fears and anxieties experienced throughout entire populations during wars. Furthermore, children who are born or raised in wartime may be particularly hardy, as well as able to endure more stresses than children who are born in times of peace and prosperity.

Major societal events like wars affect all family members. Wars restrict the timing of marriages, the availability of health care, and circumstances around the deaths of family members. Even though it is more difficult to find the usual kinds of paid work during wars, there may be new kinds of work opportunities. The everyday living conditions of families, as well as their working conditions, are highly regulated in wartime, especially when wars are fought within families' own countries.

The timing of major family events—such as geographical moves—also impacts family members' educational and work opportunities. In addition, when relatives need extensive personal care, families' social classes or financial circumstances influence whether the labor needed comes from within these families, or from paid professionals. However, even if families can afford to pay for outside helpers, this assistance is usually not available each day, or each hour of the day. This means that several family members or friends have to coordinate their caretaking labors more rigorously when a relative requires special attention.

The individual decisions that family members make around significant turning points such as births, marriages, deaths, education, and employment are greatly influenced by the historical timing of these events, and by the timing of these individuals' lives. The consequences of these decisions and events are also strongly affected by their timing. For example, if adolescents conceive a child outside marriage, the emotional stresses of raising this child as very young adults may overload or break the partners' relationship.

Particular orientations to time, which have been transmitted and used through different generations in families, have powerful influences on current family members. Sometimes a family's awareness of time is very limited, especially where family members make no attempt to link their internal family experiences to their communities or countries. When families are not thoughtful or reflective about the impact of time on their well-being, social intelligence helps us to make increasing family members' awareness of time a higher priority. Understanding the power and complexity of the influences of time in families and societies is difficult, but necessary for becoming more socially intelligent.

Significantly, families give cultural emphasis to the past, present, or future. Families who pride themselves on being traditional, for example, usually assign a great deal of importance to the past, thereby de-emphasizing the present and future. These families see the present and future as being important only insofar as they reinforce traditions of the past. As a consequence, traditionally-oriented families may not be able to assess current social conditions accurately, and their children may not be able to cope with the inevitable rough and tumble of the present.

By contrast, families who pay close attention to the present and the future tend to ignore their pasts. In so doing, they risk not honoring their families' roots. These families are more easily torn apart by the emotional overloads from looking largely to current relationships and the future for meaning and emotional security. Children in these families may become overly attached to particular peer groups, for example, because they do not see why they need relationships with their elders, or knowledge about their elders and deceased relatives. They do not understand that the past has a significant bearing on, and importance for, the quality of their present and futures.

Another example of the power and complexity of the influence of time in families is families who give their highest priority to the future. These families, often immigrants or minority groups, may appear to survive fairly well, especially if a strong shared dream guides them to improve their circumstances. Resilient families, for example, often transcend their current harsh living conditions, by clinging to ideals which they believe will ensure their successes in work worlds, or in adaptations to new countries. However, this kind of breaking away from family roots of the past is not productive in the long run. Learning to reconnect with the past and the present—as well as with the future—brings more balance, and additional emotional security, to these families.

Thus social intelligence increases our awareness of the power and complexity of time in our families. It also helps us to assess the usefulness of family orientations toward time, particularly ways in which families interpret the past, present, and future. Applying social intelligence requires that we take measures to adjust our families' biases about time for ourselves, which allows us to understand social realities from more balanced perspectives. We are objective only when we consider past, present, and future social influences in whatever we choose to do. Furthermore, the hopes we have about contributing to social justice will only be possible when we act with balanced orientations to time.

XI. Reverence for the Power and Complexity of Families

Space

When considering family behavior, space is often equated with place. However, the category of place is a more personal way of viewing and understanding the various territorial allegiances that family members have over several generations, and of explaining the specific space that families call home. For example, because family histories, local histories, and national histories are so closely intertwined, the geographical locations of most family members are fairly reliable clues to the cultures families have developed through time, families' social classes, and families' religious beliefs.

Space is a broader, more general way to think about families than place. When applying social intelligence to families, thinking in terms of space often makes it easier to be more objective about the links that exist between the different places family members are in, or have been in, and the patterns of family interaction that developed due to those places. Understanding families' uses of space is also a clearer way to assess problems of isolation—of individuals or families—which are significant in families' abilities to function.

Mapping out geographical moves, among family members in several generations of particular families, is a useful way to see patterns in place and space. Sometimes family members who migrate are stronger and more independent than family members who stay in the same place for a lifetime, for example. A crucial consequence of geographical moves in families, especially over long distances, is the differences that these moves make to significant family bonds. How do families stay in touch with each other when they are separated geographically? Can families stay emotionally connected in spite of geographical distances? Who stays connected to whom? Do family members in the original home space shun travel and contact with those relatives who left?

Changes in patterns of interaction in families inevitably follow dislocations caused by the local, national, and international migrations of family members. Social intelligence can neutralize some of the negative consequences of these dislocations, so that family well-being is not impaired by the emotional distance that frequently accompanies geographical distance. For example, we need to be especially cautious about creating situations where having fewer contacts with family members, particularly with parents or other significant family members, may lead to individual and family dysfunctions. We also need to explore, in our family histories, what impacts past migrations in our families had over several generations.

Considering the effects of space on how children are reared in our families increases our reverence for the power and complexity of our families. This focus highlights the opportunities available in families' home environments, as well as families' orientations toward these opportunities. If families withdraw from their social surroundings, for example, or establish so many community contacts that they weaken some of their family bonds, there is less balance in the perspectives transmitted to their children. Optimally we need to relate to our immediate social environments, but also to make sure that our families' roots are deep and well-connected.

Concerns about families in particular places and spaces are not focused solely on environmental social influences, but rather on family reactions to place and space. Families respond constructively, or not, to place and space issues, and social intelligence requires that we become aware of some of the difficulties families have in making these important adaptations.

Isolation is often one of the most pressing concerns that families need to deal with—in terms of their emotional relationships, family migrations, and family conflicts. Social intelligence helps us to create family emotional systems that are open and meaningfully connected to members of the entire kin group. These particular conditions are extremely significant because they prevent, or neutralize, the harmful effects of isolation.

Open, meaningful kin connections are particularly important in families that have experienced migrations, for example. Here, socially intelligent strategies include bridging gaps in family relationships that were caused by relatives' geographical moves.

XI. Reverence for the Power and Complexity of Families

However, where family conflicts—about any issues—are so intense that they precipitated geographical moves, the gaps created by these shifts are usually more difficult to bridge than dislocations caused by other kinds of migrations. This is so because the warring relatives moved away expressly to create emotional distance between themselves and the rest of their family.

Social intelligence emphasizes that geographical distance is not the same as emotional distance, and that geographical distance is not necessarily accompanied by emotional distance. If we increase the number of meaningful relationships we have in our families, we eventually open up our family emotional systems, so that geographical distance has fewer pernicious consequences for us and our relatives. In order to achieve this, we need to understand the power and complexity of place and space issues in our families. This knowledge motivates us to bridge relationship gaps in our families, which ultimately increases both family well-being and social justice.

Roles

When we define families as being made up of members who have particular roles, we oversimplify the power and complexity of our families. As human beings, we often categorize particularly complex social realities to try to control them. When we focus only on family roles, however, this simplification usually distorts family realities rather than clarifies them. For example, family roles are associated with specific behavioral expectations for being mothers, fathers, daughters, or sons. However, these conventional understandings of roles and behavior are too clear-cut and too rigid to be reliable indicators of the complex, powerful family processes that inevitably exist in families.

Considering family roles too often leads to formulating stereotypes which produce prejudice and discrimination. Simplifying the power and complexity of our families, by thinking about family roles, also leads to the construction of artificial standards which we then use to judge ourselves and others. For example, we become concerned when we cannot conform or live up to others' expectations about the family roles we assume.

Social intelligence suggests that it is much more productive for us to understand some of the power and complexity of our families, especially through considering the importance of self rather than role. Instead of examining the particular roles we think we should be playing, according to local customs, social intelligence suggests that it is more effective to see ourselves as autonomous or independent selves who are struggling to make sense of our worlds, as well as striving to build meaningful relationships with others and social justice.

This social intelligence principle—to understand the power and complexity of ourselves and our families through our observations of self and selves—gives us a more flexible baseline for appreciating the complexity of our developmental changes throughout our life-courses, as well as the systemness of our families, than focusing on family roles. Thus, rather than depending on what is ultimately a static view of our families, by examining roles, social intelligence embraces our existential struggles to stay alive and live fully by focusing on self and selves.

Merely accepting the emphases that social intelligence gives to self does not remove individual and family problems that emerge from considering families as individuals with sets of roles. However, when we accept social intelligence principles, we are less restricted by the fact that family roles necessarily give us only partial views of family realities, because they represent narrowed aspects of changing family conditions. By contrast, we benefit from thinking that selves in families are anchored by their decisions and actions, amidst their families' power and complexities, because then more realistic and more complete views of the emotional power of families emerge.

Social intelligence allows us to be more objective about our family roles, so that we see that we are frequently outside or detached from our roles. When we think of ourselves as historical actors who decide which, if any, roles we want to play, the specific norms of family roles become less powerful hard and fast rules of how to act in our rapidly changing world. Social intelligence also shows us the power and complexity of the social influences which change our role expectations, as well as the social influences that define our roles.

Applying principles of social intelligence to the power and complexity of our families requires us to be alert at all times, so that we can stay single-minded about seeing ourselves, as well as acting, amidst the difficult-to-manage mass of social influences in our families and societies. We need to be especially aware of the power and complexity of our own family emotional systems. For example, we do not become more effective as parents of an adolescent by considering conventional parental roles, but rather by understanding the major social influences in our lives, and by dealing directly with power struggles in our own families. We need all the energy and motivation we can muster to protect ourselves and others, so that we can move toward survival and fulfillment, without getting caught up in describing, explaining, and refining family roles. In most situations, collecting information only about the substance of our family roles does not necessarily increase our capacities to cope more effectively with the power and complexity of our families.

When social intelligence focuses on self, in order to understand the power and complexity of our families, it does not fragment self in the same ways that examining family roles does. Social intelligence respects the power of family roles in conventional explanations of families, but claims that the way to forge a deeper understanding of our families is to consolidate our working knowledge of self and our families' emotional systems. These emphases focus on the significance of making individual choices in our families, as well as on establishing personal and social conditions of freedom in our families and societies.

Responsibilities

An important aspect of the power and complexity of families is their moral or ethical dimensions. In some respects the traditional moral authority of families goes beyond religion, in that moral responsibility is thought of as a characteristic shared by all family members and all families. For example, in different times and different cultures, the moral authority of families is expressed through deference to family elders, whereas in modern times more specialized ethical standards, with their many ambiguities, are practiced by many families. As family members, we are often aware that family responsibilities need to be taken seriously if they are to be effective, and that each of us has to consider what our family responsibilities are.

Social intelligence emphasizes the significance of social influences which define both our enduring and changing family responsibilities. For example, our contemporary questioning of gender roles has called into question some time-bound responsibilities of men and women, sons and daughters, or mothers and fathers. We tend to live according to different moral codes and moral standards, because of social class distinctions and changing historic times. However, we also experience continuities in responsibilities through different generations, especially regarding our shared basic responsibilities for child care and the care of our elderly relatives.

In looking more closely at what goes on within our families, social intelligence shows us that divisions of labor in families imply different sets of responsibilities for young and old, or men and women. Furthermore, even though many families share the same social classes and cultures, there are wide variations about how responsibilities are assumed among families, as well as within the same families. Explorations into a particular family's history, for example, show some of the patterns of interaction that influenced who assumed responsibilities for what through time, and how effective relatives were at contributing to the overall well-being of this family and their local community.

Often parallels can be drawn between family members who assume responsibilities for other relatives, and those who contribute most to a family's well-being. However, some patterns of family interaction show dysfunctional imbalances in the sharing of responsibilities in families. For example, some family members assume more than their fair share of family responsibilities, while others evade family responsibilities. Although at present childhood and adolescence are not usually associated with assuming heavy burdens of family responsibilities, avoiding family responsibilities for a lifetime is not accepted by most families. As adults we are expected to support—financially and emotionally—ourselves and, to some extent, other family members.

When imbalances of over-responsibility and under-responsibility continue among adult family members, family dysfunctions frequently develop—sometimes among the children in a family, rather than among those adults who are not meeting their family needs responsibly. Social intelligence emphasizes the importance of understanding these family reactions if we are to be successful in improving our own functioning, as well as our families' functioning.

An effective strategy, in a situation where some family members deny family responsibilities, is to change these patterns directly by doing things differently ourselves. The family member applying principles of social intelligence to rectify imbalances in responsibilities needs to be careful not to become over-responsible. In fact, it is usually more effective to change such imbalances by becoming less responsible than usual, so that the dysfunctional balances between responsibility and irresponsibility are destabilized. The deliberate dislocation of the patterns of responsibility and irresponsibility in this family makes it is easier to redefine who does what in a new or modified division of labor.

Alternatively, in the normal course of events, sooner or later family changes or family crises occur. When a family is shaken to its roots, because of the death of a relative, for example, family members need to establish different ways to relate to each other in order to adapt to this loss. During such a period of crisis and flux or transition, social intelligence helps us to design and develop new patterns of family responsibilities, which are now more easily recognized and more readily assumed, because they are thought of as necessary for the ongoing well-being of the whole kin group.

Social intelligence also shows us how to re-establish more balanced family responsibilities in child-focused cultures and child-focused families—where children may be prized and pampered so much that they are not given sufficient family responsibilities. Social intelligence shows us that learning to assume responsibility is an important life lesson that all children need. Social intelligence also suggests that families who do not teach responsibility to their children, at young ages, do less well in life than those who encourage even the youngest children to assume some family responsibilities. For example, children who learn how to prepare food when they are young, become more independent and more aware of the needs of others, at the same time that they learn important skills that are necessary for family well-being. We all need to be needed, and this is an effective way to strengthen our senses of belonging to our families and societies.

Life

The most crucial dimension of the power and complexity of families is the life-preserving function of families. Most families support us during our most dependent stages of life—especially when we are young, old, infirm, or dying—and they help us to adapt to harsh living conditions. Perhaps families' greatest impacts on our behavior are the powerful and complex ways in which they orient us to the outside world. When we feel protected by our families, for example, we experience a strong sense of belonging, which helps us to overcome unpleasant contingencies. Ideally, however, families go beyond meeting their shared needs for security. They prepare their children and other family members to deal with the world constructively, cooperatively, and creatively.

When families are balanced, and do not have distorted emotional relationship systems, all is well in these basic overall processes. Families are able to launch their members meaningfully into societies. At the same time that family members are sufficiently free and independent to thrive in a wide variety of social settings, the original families stay intact, because family members retain a strong sense of belonging to each other, with responsible loyalties to their relatives. If families are not balanced in their emotional relationship systems, however, real and harmful distortions of these family processes occur.

Families have many ways in which they can make or break the life outcomes of their members. Social intelligence helps us to look hard at the underlying structures and dependencies in our families, so that we can ensure that we are not caught up in unproductive repetitions of negative behavior ourselves, and that we do not perpetuate behaviors that impair other family members. When we are socially intelligent, we assume family and social responsibilities to do what we can to make our families more open and more balanced, especially for the coming generations, and to increase social justice.

The ways in which social intelligence guides us to participate in our families, with greater awareness of the power and complexity of their relationship systems, strengthens us for living more fully in the wider society. Because most families have less than perfect balance and openness, increasing our social intelligence means that we make commitments to strengthen the life-enhancing powers of our families—for our own good, and for the benefit of other family members. When we realize the power and complexity of the influences that families have over our independence and freedom, we are well-situated to benefit a great deal from making this personal commitment.

Understanding the depth of conditioning that we receive from members of the different generations of our kin groups makes us realize the enormity of the task to open up our family relationship systems. This effort has to be a long-term investment, in order to achieve life-enhancing results, because short term thoughtless approaches do more harm than good. In fact, we have to be very wary about making premature moves to open up our families, because these relationships can be upset easily, and our well-intentioned actions may have undesirable consequences.

We need social intelligence to guide what we do because acting without sufficient knowledge and know-how often triggers negative results. When we have a clear sense of how our families interact, we can intervene more effectively in those patterns of behavior which affect us directly, for example. We are more adept at opening up relationship systems in our families when we participate in the usual ways in which our relatives relate to each other, than when we stand on the sidelines and guess what our relatives' particular emotions, values, and behaviors might be. There is much for us to do. When we are knowledgeable and vigilant about what we say and how we act, we make more than a satisfactory start in our long journeys to open up our family emotional systems, and to increase freedom and independence in our families and societies.

To the extent that there are sufficient conditions within families' emotional systems to encourage family members to go out into the world to make positive contributions—for example, to pursue social justice in appropriate and effective ways—these family members are immensely privileged. Some of the rewards of having stable, but lively, families are that relatives will find meaning in whatever they decide to do in their external worlds, at the same time that they continue to want to return to their families to honor them. We cannot only take from or give to our families if we are to be productive in the world.

We need to proceed as creatively as possible toward whatever community or social goals we choose, as well as to constantly renew our serious commitments to maintain openness and flexibility in our families. This dynamic tension between our family and social responsibilities strengthens the long-term power and complexity of our families, and enables us to make meaningful contributions to societies. In doing this we help to develop mature and independent family members, who will also participate meaningfully in broader communities and societies. This is the deep quality of life and family life that social intelligence promises.

Death

Families are our first teachers about death, and continue to be our best teachers about dying, death, and other kinds of loss. At best families support their family members in their grief and mourning, as well as celebrate life's joys and additions to family membership. When we either lose or add family members, patterns of family interaction that have been dormant may be activated due to the necessary stresses. However, we are also able to see our family dependencies more clearly, for example, when there are severe strains in families, such as when deaths occur and in the aftermath of significant deaths. It is more disruptive for a family to lose a much-loved relative, than to experience the addition of a child or other person to the kin group, even though these situations are also stressful to some extent.

Understanding the power and complexity of families, and increasing our reverence for the emotional bonds of our kin groups, lead us to pay close attention to how our families treat death and the consequences of deaths. When we focus on the circumstances of an actual death, and family responses to this loss, we see the extent to which families need to make effective adaptations. Ideally crises surrounding deaths—before, during, and after the deaths—are dealt with most constructively by allowing the shock to the emotional system to open up family relationships, and to resuscitate family bonds which may have been dormant for years or generations. Constructive family responses to deaths call forth intergenerational exchanges, which might not have been possible before the crisis of the death.

If families do not use the opportunities that death and loss bring to get reconnected with their kin members, schisms that already existed in these families may become more entrenched, conflicts may develop over family inheritances or resources, and family members may not be able to turn to their religions for comfort and support. These consequences occur because family crises due to deaths tend to either open up or close their family emotional systems.

Social intelligence makes us aware that we should be alert and active during all family crises, especially during periods when significant family members are dying. We need to understand as much as we possibly can about the power and complexity of our families at these times of loss, and we do this best when we place a high priority on interacting with our relatives during these critical times. In fact, the quality of our participation when relatives die is so important that family well-being, most particularly for members of the youngest generations, depends a great deal on how we handle such crises. All family members are strongly influenced by those relatives who assume responsibilities when an emotionally significant family member dies, usually more by how they conduct themselves than by what they say.

Family emotional systems are raw when deaths occur. Relatives are extremely reactive to each other during the final stages of life, as well as at the time of the death and afterwards, and it is consistently difficult for relatives to think clearly during the most critical stages of their severe losses. However, family members who are used to applying principles of social intelligence, in order to understand their families more fully, are able to be more objective and more responsible about dealing with these inevitable disruptions, than those who react only positively or negatively to what is going on around them. As in other emotionally difficult social situations, we need to be able to think clearly in order to make wise decisions and act constructively.

Social intelligence helps us to take historical perspectives on what happens around family deaths. Do families repeat their grieving rituals for all family members who die? How and why are some family members treated differently when they die? Have serious illnesses changed family attitudes toward the death of a relative? What kinds of additional losses are felt by family members because of a particular death?

XI. Reverence for the Power and Complexity of Families

Social intelligence makes us more aware of which social resources may be needed to recover from deaths in families. Do family members need grief counseling? Which family members orient relatives to what a particular death means in that family's history? Can religious rituals comfort some family members? What religious observances can be arranged for family members who want them? What particular grieving customs could be observed in a family's religion to honor the deceased relative?

Above all, social intelligence helps us to keep a positive and constructive orientation to deaths. We know that death is an integral part of life, and that we learn important lessons about life from experiencing deaths in our families. We also need to be able to transcend, to some extent, the intensity of the grief that we feel because of a death, and to see the future in terms of honoring our deceased relative.

Social intelligence gives us reverence for the power and complexity of our families, which allows us to turn wholeheartedly toward our families at times of deaths. This is a custom that has been followed throughout the ages in many societies, because it helps to heal families and their members, and not merely because it is the most socially appropriate or acceptable thing to do. We surrender ourselves to the healing processes within our families when beloved relatives die, so that we emerge more whole, as well as more inspired. Death helps us to understand new aspects of the power and complexity of our families, and increases our reverence for life.

XII. Keeping Families Important

We benefit from maintaining families as an important priority in our thinking and actions on a daily basis. When we sustain our awareness of the power and complexity of families' influences in our lives—and in societies—at all times, we incorporate this into our decisions and actions. Giving these emotional powerhouses our attention makes our families more likely to relinquish their capacities to control what and how we contribute to others.

Keeping families a high priority in our everyday considerations does not mean that we become slaves to our families, but rather that we work at gaining more freedom to act constructively. When our families are a high priority, we interact more meaningfully within our families, as well as make more substantial contributions to our families and communities. When we are socially intelligent, our families serve as our anchors, but at the same time we cultivate flexible bonds with our relatives. This means that we can come and go with some degree of ease and freedom in our families, in spite of the power and tenacity of these emotional bonds.

Building social intelligence depends on continuing to increase our awareness of the importance of families—our own and others' families. Families do not have general moral importance as much as pragmatic, emotional significance, which leads to our survival, adaptation, and fulfillment, as well as to increased social justice. Families are our launching pads, and strong societies need to be able to build effective families if we are to enjoy the fruits of our civilizations.

Social intelligence shows us that keeping families important is not an end in itself, but rather a means to an end. We cannot live satisfactorily only within our families, and to be fully alive means that we have to mature and assume responsibilities for conditions within our societies as well as within our families. Our families prepare us for these broader ventures, as well as orient us to understand and act in the world around us.

Being fully awake to the many opportunities we have, to contribute to communities and societies, requires that we continue to assess the emotional hold our families have on our thinking and actions. Accepting the power and complexity of our families necessitates coming to terms with their ongoing restrictiveness. One of the most meaningful ways to accomplish this is to commit ourselves to work toward increasing freedom within our families as much as we can. However, opening up our family emotional systems is difficult and demanding, and we need to know our families well in order to intervene in these powerful processes responsibly and effectively.

Being socially intelligent requires us to continue to learn about the ongoing impacts of our families and other powerful social influences: beliefs, social classes, cultures, and societies. We cannot be satisfied by using only narrow perspectives to understand our lives, no matter how much economic and cultural values bestow social honor on achieving refined specializations. Artificially restricted perspectives distort objective realities, whereas the broad base of social intelligence rings true. Applying the broad views of social intelligence to our everyday lives allows us to put our priorities and goals in meaningful and realistic contexts. By contrast, continuing to use the narrow perspectives of specializations limits our understanding of social problems and social issues that could otherwise be resolved, at least to some extent.

Continuing to learn about our families, as well as families in different societies, makes us aware of the omnipresence of families—in our beliefs, social classes, cultures, and societies.

XII. Keeping Families Important

Only when we locate families in these different spheres of major social influences do we fully understand them, and only then are we sufficiently free to make commitments to work toward social justice.

Part of the power and complexity of families is due to the fact that some of our most important family bonds are invisible. Even though we cannot easily measure the effects of our family connections and relationships beyond the here and now, their influences persist. We scratch the surface of these powerful and complex bonds by examining current patterns in family behavior, especially those that are repeated through different generations and in different social classes, and by intervening to increase their constructive impacts.

Following our intuitions does not work well in the long run, because this kind of automatic behavior tends to reproduce what already exists. We need to be able to think clearly about our present conditions, as well as about our options for change, if we are to be innovative. We establish our most meaningful priorities when we base them on our knowledge of the power of social influences, because these forces control critical human potentials and limitations. In these ways we make choices that carry us forward. Social intelligence is a reliable fund of knowledge which guides us toward making the most of whatever we choose to do.

Continuing to Learn about Families

Social intelligence is an asset which needs constant expansion, reinforcement, and renewal. The benefit of having and using a heightened social awareness, in how we think and what we do, is hard-won. In order to achieve this, we have to continuously open our minds to new facts, and to the deeper understanding that broad social perspectives bring. A true education in social intelligence both broadens and deepens our understanding, which requires that we constantly examine and question what we take for granted, as well as the knowledge that we use in our everyday lives.

Because social intelligence requires these continuities, we realize that social intelligence is not a static or a contained resource. We are neither born with the kind of social intelligence that serves us for a lifetime, nor do we reach a particular level of social intelligence where we do not need to continue to learn about the power and complexity of social influences. Thus, when we make a commitment to increase our social intelligence, we must also make a lifetime commitment to increase it.

If this agenda sounds unrealistic, or too demanding, we should consider the opposite. When we choose not to continue to learn about our families, for example, we become more or less pawns in the strong emotional processes of our families, whereby we lose our independence and freedom. Not continuing to learn about our families, in terms of assessing their impacts on how we think and act, necessarily decreases our social intelligence, so that we predictably do less well in life.

If it is too difficult to make commitments to try to examine and understand our families through the principles of social intelligence, we can perhaps at least suspend our judgments about the usefulness of social intelligence in our families, until we have made substantial numbers of applications of social intelligence in our thinking and behavior. Experiencing the changes that occur, when our thoughts and actions are guided by the new perspectives of social intelligence, may eventually convince us that this is the way to go.

One fact to consider, in taking this trial and error approach to applying social intelligence in our families, is that increasing our social intelligence—in any social context, but more particularly in our families—calls forth deep, challenging, and difficult processes, by examining social emotions and some of the most basic assumptions we make about ourselves, our families, and society. Social intelligence does not present easy solutions or quick fixes to problematic situations. Rather, social intelligence inspires us with new perspectives and new ideas, and makes possible more meaningful commitments to express our most cherished ideals and values in increasing social justice.

In order to accomplish these goals, we need to learn about our families in a spirit of open inquiry, with as much objectivity as possible. We should also be prepared to change our ideas, whenever our habitual strategies in our families do not work well. In these ways we become researchers, because we compare our findings about our families with social trends in families, and with whatever we see and understand about other families in communities, societies, and globalization. Our efforts to apply social intelligence principles include integrating these different ways of seeing families, with what we do on a daily basis in our own families.

Even though these tasks are challenging, we can do something constructive each day, so that we proceed in a spirit of refining how we interact with our families, in order to eventually accomplish what we want—not only with our families, but also in societies. This process can give us sufficient energy and motivation for a lifetime, so we experience more meaningful fulfillment, and make more real contributions to social justice than would otherwise be possible.

When our family responsibilities and tasks are pared down to workable dimensions, we are more selective and more effective in applying social intelligence principles to the major social influences in and on our families. We consider particularly, and selectively, for example, how our families are in relation to others' families, beliefs, social classes, cultures, and societies. Social intelligence reveals the omnipresence of families in societies, and inspires us to base our learning about families on understanding how we can make constructive differences in them. In this way we continue to learn about the power and complexity of our families, in order to be more knowledgeable, and in order to develop the kind of empathy that will increase the common good.

Finding Families in Beliefs

We necessarily become social researchers through our endeavors to be more socially intelligent. One of our basic tasks in increasing our social intelligence is to assess the meanings of our most important beliefs—especially about our families—that infiltrate and permeate our daily lives. We do this because it is much easier, and more practical, to get a clear idea of the impact of these beliefs when we see how they influence our thinking. Beliefs are particularly important because they have social origins—How did we get the beliefs we have?—and because they influence how we behave.

One of the clearest connections between our families and our beliefs is the extent to which we are believers in particular religions, and how religions influence our faith about issues such as our family responsibilities and our understanding of human nature, life on earth, and life after death. Religious beliefs frequently determine whether we tend to be active or passive in our orientations to life, for example. Do we believe that it is more responsible to act according to our own initiatives, or do we wait for divine inspiration by letting events unfold?

Religions can influence all of life's activities if we choose to follow the details of their traditions. One of the keys in assessing the influence of religious beliefs in our own lives is to see whether or not we call upon religious guidance for most of our activities, or for relatively few. To what extent do we depend on divine guidance in our decision-making and day-to-day behavior? Do our families follow religious traditions closely? Do we benefit directly from these beliefs and our related actions?

Our beliefs may include several sets of beliefs, as well as fairly random beliefs which do not co-ordinate comfortably. Some of us are riddled with contradictory beliefs, which are essentially at war with each other, so that our behavior may seem to be random rather than guided by particular beliefs. Others are not aware of the beliefs they have. Because of these widespread conditions, increasing our social intelligence is an important way to sort out what we really believe, and how useful these beliefs are, for our well-being and for the well-being of others.

The process of sifting through our beliefs, and editing them for their constructive content and consequences, can be upsetting. This is not a fly-by-night project, which can be completed quickly and then put to one side. It is a lifetime endeavor which influences the way our lives turn out, so it has to be treated with care, sensitivity, and seriousness. Social intelligence requires that we not only know what our beliefs are, but also which are the strongest and most powerful, because it is our strongest beliefs that have the most far-reaching consequences as orientations to our behavior and life itself.

Some sets of beliefs, which have strong impacts on what we do in our families, are our political beliefs, our beliefs in education and science, our environmental beliefs, and our beliefs in human nature. As with our religious beliefs, it is important to know the content or substance of these beliefs. What kinds of political ideologies do we believe in? What kinds of governments do we prefer? How are our families affected by our political beliefs? Who gave us our beliefs in the importance of education, science, and the environment? When we see how our beliefs were transmitted to us, it becomes easier to connect them with our families, and easier to change them. We were not born with beliefs—they result from particular social processes, most especially from patterns in our families' interactions.

Our political beliefs not only support or protest the ways in which governments distribute their resources, but they also define the extent to which we and our families encourage relatives to participate in significant political decision-making. Democracies vary according to whether citizens are real players in political processes that define the common good of societies. For example, when we believe in particular political parties, we accept specific ways of thinking, doing, and accomplishing the common good. Thus our capacities and effectiveness in working toward the common good are either increased or restricted by our political beliefs, as well as by our family processes.

Our beliefs in education and science also liberate us—by encouraging us to learn—or restrict us—by questioning the benefits of either education or science. Our acceptance of social intelligence is influenced by these beliefs, and we ultimately reject social intelligence when we do not believe in the importance of learning. It is important to see how we received our beliefs about education and science, especially if we want to change them. Furthermore, our lives open up if we move from belittling education and science, for example, to respecting them and using them in our lives.

Environmental beliefs include wide ranges of views, including less destructive ways of eating, as well as how we use or abuse our environmental resources. These broad beliefs give us world views, which sometimes channel our political actions toward relatively narrow ideals and goals. Environmental activism encourages action rather than passivity, for example, but frequently to accomplish fairly narrow or limited goals. However, because all environmental beliefs are rooted in social systems, they are inevitably major mechanisms of social change, as well as sources of varied commitments to increase social justice.

Some of our most general beliefs, such as our beliefs in human nature, have powerful influences on how we think about ourselves, our families, our communities, and our societies. Specific belief systems, such as religious or political beliefs, also address beliefs in human nature either explicitly or implicitly. Often we need to probe to discover what our beliefs in human nature are, through examining both our general and specific belief systems. When we understand more fully how we think about human nature and human potential, we see that social intelligence calls into question all beliefs which do not accept the power of learning, as well as encourages us to embrace ideals that help us to build stronger families and stronger societies.

XII. Keeping Families Important

Finding Families in Social Classes

Families are not only ever-present in our beliefs, and in the beliefs of others, but they also permeate our understanding of social classes. In fact, social classes are conventionally thought of as being composed of families, rather than individuals, even though this way of looking at social class memberships may not be accurate or realistic.

We search for families in social classes with the social intelligence starting point that family components of social classes are just as strong as family components of beliefs. Even though family concerns within and among social classes may be more hidden from view than families in our beliefs, they are there. Families are present in all social classes, whether our understanding of social class is based on economic means, educational achievement, gender, sexual orientation, race, ethnicity, or able-bodiedness.

Although the emotional systems of families override the importance of individual family members' social class affiliations, most families either place themselves—or are placed by others—in particular social classes as whole families. Thus a family unit claims, or is given, a particular social class membership, even though there may be discrepancies between how most family members see themselves in relation to social classes, and how others assign social classes to them.

In these respects a special kind of emotional family unity exists—family unity is thrust upon families by their own members, as well as by visible or invisible others who assign social classes to them. Social intelligence suggests that although many of us conform to others' definitions of social class statuses, individual family members are responsible for carving out their own class memberships, regardless of how relatives or family outsiders see them as belonging to particular social classes. Even though being thought of as members of social classes is largely an inescapable social reality, social intelligence emphasizes that it is better to make choices about our own class identities, than to be assigned social classes by others.

Families and Social Intelligence

Conventional thinking about families and social classes suggests that families often meet the needs of particular social classes. When a family tries to move from a low social class to a middle social class, for example, this may be possible only if their children, or some of their young adults, conform to standards set by members of the middle classes. If the base of these social classes is economic, the low class family must do whatever it takes to amass sufficient economic means to be considered—by middle class members—to belong to the middle class.

Upward mobility in social classes, which base their membership on educational achievement, shows similar patterns. Families wanting to move from low to middle social classes have to provide well-established, improved levels of educational accomplishment for their youngest family members, in order to gradually gain the required middle class members' social acceptance. However, where social classes are based on physiological differences—such as gender, sexual orientation, race, or able-bodiedness—upward mobility from lower to middle classes cannot be as easily won, because families usually cannot change their physiological characteristics.

Adaptations which achieve social mobility in classes based on physiological differences include lower class family members who successfully pass for mainstream middle classes, by masking their physiological differences, or by amassing both economic means and educational credentials. A more authentic, fail-proof method, however, is to use social intelligence as a guide for changing our own individual behavior. When families or individual family members understand the power and complexity of social classes, and their strong impacts on our lives, they can refuse to conform to social class pressures. This socially intelligent strategy is a useful neutralizing factor for all families and individuals. We realize that social classes, although frequently hidden, have strong influences on our life-outcomes, but we can also decide to do whatever we can to resist or negate being defined by the social classes that others assign to us.

XII. Keeping Families Important

When, as individuals or as families, we act in ways which are not defined by social class expectations, we claim an all-important freedom. Before we can do this successfully, however, we need to be aware of how significant social class influences are for our families. When we have this knowledge, we can more effectively neutralize social class influences on our everyday situations. Although it takes a while to loosen the grip that social classes have on us—and on our families' thinking, being, and doing—this effort is worthwhile. When we withstand social class pressures, we become stronger examples of social intelligence to other family members, who then follow suit and gain their own freedoms.

Seeing Families in Cultures

We keep families sufficiently important in our day-to-day lives when we pay attention to family themes in our cultures. These may be accounts of actual or imagined ways of being in our families, or they may be symbolic representations in fine arts, television, movies, or magazines. Whatever ways we see families portrayed in our cultures, we learn something new about how families are—or are imagined to be—as well as how people want their families to be, from these cultural sources.

In order to be reasonably objective, or critical, about cultural representations of families, which swamp us at every turn, we must continue to increase our social intelligence, as well as our knowledge and understanding of families. For example, when we watch theatrical presentations of family crises, we often see interesting and sometimes fairly accurate views of how family emotional systems work. Also, when we see cultural contrasts in the importance of elders in families, for example, by deliberately going beyond our own Western cultural experiences, we understand more fully how family behaviors are passed down from generation to generation through our own cultures. Wide varieties of cultural contrasts in families strengthen our objectivity, and clarify our ideas about how family members respond when they are caught up in their reactive family emotional systems.

219

We also increase our awareness of families in cultures when we pick up as much implied information about families as we can. Social expectations about families are not always articulated clearly by our cultures, so we need to read between the lines of communications and family imagery, in order to estimate how much power our families have over our ideas and behavior. Do we honor our families with financial resources, or with empty rhetoric? Do we praise mothers, but at the same time make their lives extraordinarily difficult and stressful?

Our cultures are rich with examples of how we deal with family births, illnesses, and deaths, including descriptions of what we are expected to feel, and how we are expected to act in critical family situations. This broad cultural knowledge of families increases our social intelligence, and makes it a more effective guide in decisions about what we really want to accomplish for our families and societies. When we want to start our own nuclear families, for example, do we decide to go along with cultural expectations for our social classes, or do we decide to do things differently?

These decisions of whether or not to conform to cultural expectations are important. We make such decisions freely and wisely only when we understand what the price is that we pay for nonconformity. Societies develop cultures essentially to increase families' and individuals' conformity to particular standards, because societies cannot exist without the widespread acceptance of specific cultural values. When we choose not to conform to certain family or cultural expectations, our behaviors are inevitably sanctioned negatively, which may be as mild as social disapproval, or as harsh as arrest and imprisonment. The waters of our cultures run deep, and there is a remarkably strong cultural consensus that some family values and standards must be upheld in order to meet the survival needs of our families and our societies.

We increase our awe for the power and complexity of our families by examining the myriad nuances and expectations in our cultures which reflect the basic missions that families still have in modern societies. Increased varieties of families show us that families remain important and significant in societies, because they continue to provide optimal conditions for the procreation and socialization of our children, as well as meet dependency and companionship needs.

Social intelligence incorporates the fact that considerable numbers of people do not accept society's agenda to give birth and rear children of their own. However, as human beings, most of us continue to have needs for the kind of intimacy and companionship that diverse families provide. Even though meaningful, and sometimes hardy, family substitutes have emerged in our cultures, multigenerational families—which are linked to countless past generations—remain powerful, especially when we become more aware of cross-cultural contrasts among families in international cultures. Multigenerational families provide us with the most adequate opportunities to participate directly in our personal ties to the distant past. This compelling power of multigenerational families, through both time and space, makes them unique and unlike other small groups.

Seeing Families in Societies

When we use the broadest social perspective, societies, to look at the social contexts of our families, we become even more detached and more objective in our understanding of them. Now we see not only our own family emotional systems, but also other societies' patterns of family interactions, and ways of doing things through their families. When we use these broad social contexts to see families, we identify their more widespread patterns of behavior. Such an overview helps us to clarify which family trends and characteristics we want, or do not want to have, in our own families.

We understand more fully the importance of having flexibility in our family relationships, as well as freedom throughout our families, when we compare families in a number of contrasting societies. Comparisons are effective ways to understand our families more deeply, whether they are made among a few individual families, or among many families in different societies. We start to think more clearly about our own families when we are able to understand what other families are like, for example, as well as when we see important nuances in variations of family forms and processes.

We realize the power and complexity of our own families when we recognize and understand broad social trends in families. This strategy also helps us to keep our families important, because paying attention to the everyday details of our own families is not enough. Fragmented, specific views of our families are inevitably subjective, and we cannot easily step back from them to compare and contrast our families with other families from this vantage point. When we use social intelligence to consider our families from societal perspectives, however, our deeper learning about families yields new meanings. Being socially intelligent about our families requires us to continue to educate ourselves by examining families in societies, which deepens our appreciation of families' emotional and interactive powers.

Strengthening our capacities to see families in societies helps us to recognize their presence and pervasiveness in everything we do, and to realize the importance of paying attention to the power of invisible kin groups in how we conduct ourselves. We see some of the ways in which our individual family histories fit with the histories of societies, for example, and we see links among families which connect them to the welfare, wellbeing, and outcomes of different families in the same historical contexts. Just as nuclear families are inextricably connected to their kin groups, all families have some effects on each other, especially when they are in similar social classes.

These complex relationships are only apparent when we pay attention to families in societies. Such broad views are more than new perspectives, or new ways to learn about our families and their roles in the well-being of our societies. Placing our families in societal contexts increases our objectivity about our families, which enhances our capacities to think clearly and gain freedom.

XII. Keeping Families Important

Ultimately we need to keep families important in our everyday lives, so that their power does not overwhelm us. The power and complexity of families is no respecter of persons. Women, men, young, old, and dependent or independent adults are all vulnerable to being controlled by family emotional processes, even though some family members may appear to be more dominant than others in their families. When we understand more about families in societies, as well as in personal terms, our increased objectivity helps us to see how family dependencies and loyalties can prevent us from living fully, or from having secure emotional bases.

Seeing and understanding families in societies increase our independence in our families, and in coping with our everyday family responsibilities. Increasing our objectivity and social intelligence gives us more satisfactory ways to meet shared family needs. For example, we appreciate more vividly why each family member has the right to live fully, and we are more motivated to do whatever we can to accomplish this, for ourselves and for other relatives. Once we cope effectively with our family needs, we become sufficiently free to consider more seriously how we can make differences in societies.

If we choose to use our heightened awareness about our families and societies for selfish goals, such as financial gain through exploiting others, we still have much to learn about family emotional systems and the systemness of other social groups. Also, if we decide not to cultivate social intelligence through doing things differently, we will be increasingly vulnerable to the damaging aspects of our family emotional systems—we cannot cultivate openness merely through learning about social realities. We must therefore decide to increase our social intelligence about our families, through our actions as well as through our thinking, if we want to have full and rewarding lives.

Investing Emotions in Social Justice

When we let social intelligence guide us in getting to know how our families anchor our being and actions, we get stronger in our exchanges with others, and more idealistic—yet practical—in our goals. We are more in charge of who we are, what we want to accomplish, and how we want to be in the world. Furthermore, when we heighten our historical awareness, we see what needs to be done to make our families stronger, and how the world could change in more constructive ways.

Part of establishing this momentum for ourselves includes improving our understanding of social justice, and applying the principles of social intelligence to social problems as well as to ourselves and our families. Human purposes are greater than strengthening who we are, and how our families interact. We have responsibilities to act on behalf of those who cannot articulate their own best interests, or who do not know how to express their concerns in powerful historical changes.

One of the ways in which we get sufficiently motivated to do this work, and sustain our motivations, is to choose to invest our emotions and energies differently. When we connect how we act with our family emotional systems, we loosen the grip that intergenerational patterns of behavior have over us. This allows us to apply our emotional energies to tasks other than repeating the expectations and behaviors that have been passed down in our families through time.

When we change our parts in the emotional reactions of the chains of repeated events in our families, we establish new ways to interact with our relatives and, consequently, in other social settings. Because principles of social intelligence guide our actions, we act not only with a sound knowledge of interpersonal influences within our families, but also with awareness of the power that beliefs, social classes, cultures, and societies have over us and our families. We learn to practice applying these perspectives in all that we do, which gradually allows us to invest more of our energies in social justice issues.

These new patterns of behavior establish new directions for a lifetime. We realize that we cannot go back to how we used to behave—in spite of others' pressures to do so—without decreasing our social intelligence. Furthermore, once we have seen ourselves, our families, and the world according to social intelligence, we no longer want to return to our previous priorities and ways of doing things.

Our missions to work toward increasing social justice are often not moral issues, but rather practical ways of being in the world. As we apply principles of social intelligence, we become more aware of our individual and social responsibilities, which include trying to make the world a better place. Our family know-how eventually shows us that we have obligations to establish conditions of freedom in the world, as well as in our families, and we do this to protect ourselves, and to assist those who cannot help themselves.

An important lesson we learn from our families is the nature of human nature, and the scope of human potential. First we see the destructive consequences that family emotional systems may have on diminishing our lives. Then, as we work to loosen the grip of these negative influences, we see what life can be. Even though we may accomplish no more than a few changes in our usual ways of doing things, these will make marked differences in how we act in relation to our families and others, and in how we proceed with our lives.

Coming to grips with the power and complexity of our families is a significant step toward investing our emotions in social justice. Even though the initial stages of learning about our family emotional processes are difficult, challenging, and even harrowing, the overall purpose of struggling to free ourselves is to invest more fully in ways to increase social justice. We stay the course, however taxing, because we know at a deep level that these goals are worthwhile. Eventually we gain the privilege of leading a more meaningful life, and we see how we and others increase self-respect, and sometimes social honor, by moving in similar directions. These actions keep our family relationships open and balanced, so that members of the next generations are sufficiently strong to contribute to their and others' worlds.

Suggested Reading

Baca Zinn, Maxine, and Stanley Eitzen. 2005. *Diversity in American Families*, 7th ed. New York: Allyn and Bacon.

Barton, Jane Hughes. 1994. *Remarriage after 50: What Women, Men and Adult Children Need to Know*. New York: Roger Thomas Press.

Bowen, Murray. 1978. *Family Therapy in Clinical Practice*. New York: Jason Aronson.

Cherlin, Andrew. 1999. *Public and Private Families*. Boston: McGraw Hill.

Coontz, Stephanie. 1997. *The Way We Really Are: Coming to Terms with America's Changing Families*. New York: Basic Books.

DeVault, Marjorie L. 1991. *Feeding the Family: The Social Organization of Caring as Gendered Work*. Chicago: University of Chicago Press.

Gardner, Howard. 1983. *Multiple Intelligences*. New York: Basic Books.

Giddens, Anthony. 1999. *Runaway World: How Globalization is Shaping Our Lives*. London: Profile Books.

Goleman, Daniel. 1995. *Emotional Intelligence: Why It Can Matter More Than IQ*. New York: Bantam Books.

Goode, William J. 1970. *World Revolution and Family Patterns.* New York: Free Press.

Hall, C. Margaret. 1994. *New Families: Reviving and Creating Meaningful Bonds.* New York: Haworth.

Hall, C. Margaret. 1999. *The Special Mission of Grandparents: Hearing, Seeing, Telling.* Westport, CT: Bergin & Garvey.

Kerr, Michael E., and Murray Bowen. 1988. *Family Evaluation.* New York: W. W. Norton.

Millman, Marcia. 1991. *Warm Hearts and Cold Cash: The Intimate Dynamics of Families and Money.* New York: Free Press.

Mills, C. Wright. 1959. *The Sociological Imagination.* New York: Oxford University Press.

Mintz, Steven, and Susan Kellogg. 1988. *Domestic Revolutions: A Social History of American Family Life.* New York: Free Press.

Risman, Barbara J. 1998. *Gender Vertigo: American Families in Transition.* New Haven, CT: Yale University Press.

Rochelle, Ann. 1997. *No More Kin: Exploring Race, Class, and Gender in Family Networks.* Thousand Oaks, CA: Pine Forge.

Stacey, Judith. 1990. *Brave New Families: Stories of Domestic Upheaval in Late Twentieth-Century America.* New York: Basic Books.

Tumin, Melvin. 1973. *Patterns of Society.* Boston: Little, Brown.

Voydanoff, Patricia. 1987. *Work and Family Life*. Beverly Hills, CA: Sage.

Weeks, Jeffrey, Brian Heaphy, and Catherine Donovan. 2001. *Same Sex Intimacies: Families of Choice and Other Life Experiments*. New York: Routledge.

With many thanks to my colleagues at Georgetown University Sociology and Anthropology Department, the Bowen Center for the Study of the Family, Sociological Practice Association, Society for Applied Sociology, Association for Applied and Clinical Sociology, and the Commission on Applied and Clinical Sociology. I am also indebted to my clients and students, who have taught me so much, and of course to my wonderful American and English families, who continue to put up with me on a daily basis.

www.ingramcontent.com/pod-product-compliance
Lightning Source LLC
Chambersburg PA
CBHW060243290526
45789CB00001B/174